HOUGHTON MIFFLIN

# Treasure

INVITATIONS
TO LITERACY

**Houghton Mifflin Company • Boston**

Atlanta • Dallas • Geneva, Illinois • Palo Alto • Princeton

HOUGHTON MIFFLIN

# Treasure

**Senior Authors**

J. David Cooper
John J. Pikulski

**Authors**

Kathryn H. Au
Margarita Calderón
Jacqueline C. Comas
Marjorie Y. Lipson
J. Sabrina Mims
Susan E. Page
Sheila W. Valencia
MaryEllen Vogt

**Consultants**

Dolores Malcolm
Tina Saldivar
Shane Templeton

INVITATIONS TO LITERACY

**Houghton Mifflin Company • Boston**

Atlanta • Dallas • Geneva, Illinois • Palo Alto • Princeton

Cover and title page photography by Tim Turner.

Cover illustration from *Too Many Tamales*, by Gary Soto, illustrated by
Ed Martinez.  Illustration copyright © 1993 by Ed Martinez.
Reprinted by permission of G.P. Putnam's Sons.

Acknowledgments appear on page 285.

Printed in the U.S.A.

ISBN: 0-395-79499-4

56789-VH-98 97

## Themes

# Family Photos

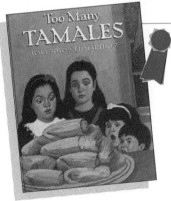

# CONTENTS

THAT'S INCREDIBLE!

**BIG BOOK PLUS**

## Anthology

# Tell Me a Tale

**BIG BOOK PLUS**

**Bringing the Rain to Kapiti Plain**
a folktale retold by Verna Aardema
illustrated by Beatriz Vidal

**In the same book . . .**
photos of the Serengeti Plain, zebra
questions and answers, and a zebra poem

## Anthology

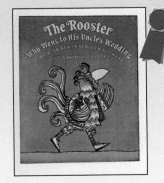

# Family Photos

Clean Your Room,
Harvey Moon!
*by Pat Cummings*

# Table of Contents

WATCH **ME** READ

**The Wish Broom**

WATCH **ME** READ

**A Bigger Family**

WATCH **ME** READ

**Jenny's Far-Away Family**

WATCH **ME** READ

**Wait a Second**

PAPERBACK **PLUS**

Amelia Bedelia's Family Album

Pictures by LYNN SWEAT

**More Books You Can Read!**

# Meet Vera B. Williams

When I was a child, my hard-working mother decided we had to buy *one* comfortable chair. The chair cost a lot of money, and my family worried about that. It spoiled the joy of having a new chair.

But the chair in the story is an imagined chair. I painted it with the richest of reds so my character could sit in it with her mother and not have to worry at all.

My mother works as a waitress in the Blue Tile Diner. After school sometimes I go to meet her there. Then her boss Josephine gives me a job too. I wash the salts and peppers and fill the ketchups. One time I peeled all the onions for the onion soup. When I finish, Josephine says, "Good work, honey," and pays me. And every time, I put half of my money into the jar.

It takes a long time to fill a jar this big. Every day when my mother comes home from work, I take down the jar. My mama empties all her change from tips out of her purse for me to count. Then we push all of the coins into the jar.

Sometimes my mama is laughing when she comes home from work. Sometimes she's so tired she falls asleep while I count the money out into piles. Some days she has lots of tips. Some days she has only a little. Then she looks worried. But each evening every single shiny coin goes into the jar.

We sit in the kitchen to count the tips. Usually Grandma sits with us too. While we count, she likes to hum. Often she has money in her old leather wallet for us. Whenever she gets a good bargain on tomatoes or bananas or something she buys, she puts by the savings and they go into the jar.

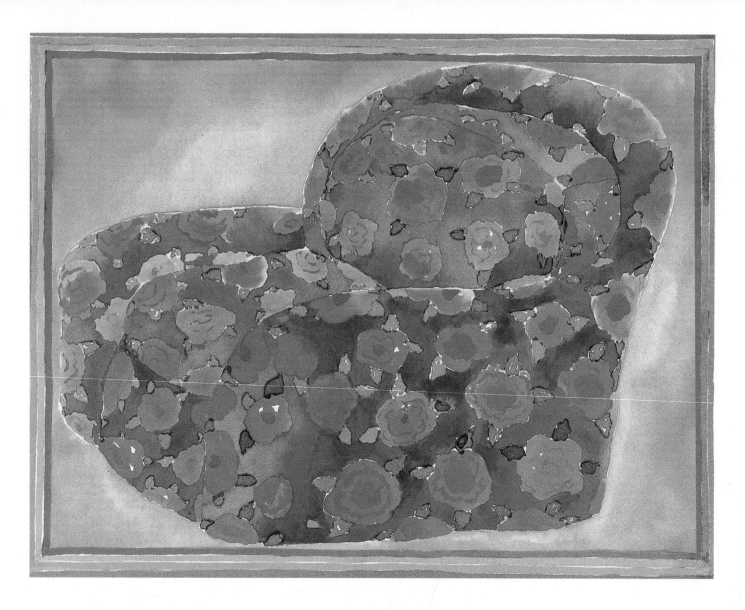

When we can't get a single other coin into the jar, we are going to take out all the money and go and buy a chair.

Yes, a chair. A wonderful, beautiful, fat, soft armchair. We will get one covered in velvet with roses all over it. We are going to get the best chair in the whole world.

That is because our old chairs burned up. There was a big fire in our other house. All our chairs burned. So did our sofa and so did everything else. That wasn't such a long time ago.

My mother and I were coming home from buying
new shoes. I had new sandals. She had new pumps. We were
walking to our house from the bus. We were looking at
everyone's tulips. She was saying she liked red tulips and
I was saying I liked yellow ones. Then we came to our block.

Right outside our house stood two big fire engines. I could see lots of smoke. Tall orange flames came out of the roof. All the neighbors stood in a bunch across the street. Mama grabbed my hand and we ran. My uncle Sandy saw us and ran to us. Mama yelled, "Where's Mother?" I yelled, "Where's my grandma?" My aunt Ida waved and shouted, "She's here, she's here. She's O.K. Don't worry."

Grandma was all right. Our cat was safe too, though it took a while to find her. But everything else in our whole house was spoiled.

What was left of the house was turned to charcoal and ashes.

We went to stay with my mother's sister Aunt Ida and Uncle Sandy. Then we were able to move into the apartment downstairs. We painted the walls yellow. The floors were all shiny. But the rooms were very empty.

The first day we moved in, the neighbors brought pizza and cake and ice cream. And they brought a lot of other things too.

The family across the street brought a table and three kitchen chairs. The very old man next door gave us a bed from when his children were little.

My other grandpa brought us his beautiful rug. My mother's other sister, Sally, had made us red and white

curtains. Mama's boss, Josephine, brought pots and pans,
silverware and dishes. My cousin brought me her own
stuffed bear.

Everyone clapped when my grandma made a speech.
"You are all the kindest people," she said, "and we thank
you very, very much. It's lucky we're young and can start
all over."

That was last year, but we still have no sofa and no big chairs. When Mama comes home, her feet hurt. "There's no good place for me to take a load off my feet," she says. When Grandma wants to sit back and hum and cut up potatoes, she has to get as comfortable as she can on a hard kitchen chair.

So that is how come Mama brought home the biggest jar she could find at the diner and all the coins started to go into the jar.

Now the jar is too heavy for me to lift down. Uncle Sandy gave me a quarter. He had to boost me up so I could put it in.

After supper Mama and Grandma and I stood in front of the
jar. "Well, I never would have believed it, but I guess it's full,"
Mama said.

My mother brought home little paper wrappers for the
nickels and the dimes and the quarters. I counted them all out
and wrapped them all up.

On my mother's day off, we took all the coins to the bank.
The bank exchanged them for ten-dollar bills. Then we took
the bus downtown to shop for our chair.

We shopped through four furniture stores. We tried out
big chairs and smaller ones, high chairs and low chairs, soft
chairs and harder ones. Grandma said she felt like Goldilocks
in "The Three Bears" trying out all the chairs.

Finally we found the chair we were all dreaming of. And
the money in the jar was enough to pay for it. We called Aunt
Ida and Uncle Sandy. They came right down in their pickup
truck to drive the chair home for us. They knew we couldn't
wait for it to be delivered.

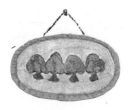

I tried out our chair in the back of the truck. Mama
wouldn't let me sit there while we drove. But they let me sit
in it while they carried it up to the door.

We set the chair right beside the window with the red and white curtains. Grandma and Mama and I all sat in it while Aunt Ida took our picture.

Now Grandma sits in it and talks with people going by in the daytime. Mama sits down and watches the news on TV when she comes home from her job. After supper, I sit with her and she can reach right up and turn out the light if I fall asleep in her lap.

34

# Picture This

Aunt Ida took a picture of the family sitting in their new chair. This picture might go in their family album. Draw some other pictures for the family's album. Then choose a way to share your ideas.

- Write a sentence or two about each picture.
- Tell a friend about the pictures.

# My Trip to Shay Lake

## A True Story by Stephanie Davis

Stephanie had an exciting day at Shay Lake!
She wanted to share her fun, so she
wrote about her trip.

### My Trip to Shay Lake

One bright morning around seven o'clock my dad, my mom, my sister, and I were getting ready to go to our cabin at Shay Lake.

We packed my mom's van with our clothes, food, and our fishing equipment. It took us about two hours to get there.

When we got there, my dad, my sister, and I gathered the bait, the fishing poles, and the pail and walked down to the lake. We sat down and put our bait on our fishing poles. I threw my fishing line in the water and nothing happened. My sister and my dad put their fishing lines in the water also, but still nothing happened.

My sister, Crystal, asked, "When will the fish come?"

I said, "Soon, Crystal. You have to be real quiet and then the fish will come to eat the bait."

All of a sudden the fish ate my bait. I said, "Dad, I think I have a fish!"

He said, "O.K. Hold the pole still, and I will help you pull it out." He came over and pulled my line out of the water. There was a big fish on it.

Crystal said, "You have a big fish, Stephanie!"

I said, "Wow! I want to do this again!"

We couldn't wait to tell Mom about our exciting day. Crystal was so excited she did most of the talking. I can't wait to go to Shay Lake next summer.

*Stephanie Davis*
*Mae C. Jemison Academy*
*Detroit, Michigan*

*Stephanie wrote this story when she was in the second grade. She chose this idea to write about because she likes to fish. Stephanie also likes movies and karate. She would like to become an astronaut someday.*

37

# Families in Art

*Rocking Chair Number 3 by Henry Moore*

*To Friendship by Mr. Amos Ferguson*

Maureen

Judie

Joe

Tomie

Tomie when he was a boy with his brother and sisters.

Tomie now

40

# Meet Tomie dePaola

The story you are about to read is based on something that really happened. My grandfather, Tom, had a stroke just like Bob in the story. I was a grownup though, and my grandfather didn't get better. But the part about the blocks is real. If you came to visit me, you'd see them on a shelf in my living room.

I actually use my memory of things that happened in my family in other books of mine too. *Nana Upstairs & Nana Downstairs* is a true story. It's about the special friendship I had with my 94-year-old great-grandmother, Nana Upstairs, when I was very young.

*The Art Lesson* is about something that really happened to me in school. I changed the name of my kindergarten and first grade teachers, but all of the other names, including the art teacher, are real.

*Tom* is about my Irish grandfather. He was so much fun, and after Nana Upstairs died, he was my best friend. He was always getting me into trouble — not serious trouble, though. When you read this book, you'll understand what I mean.

There are still some stories that I'm writing that are about other members of my family.

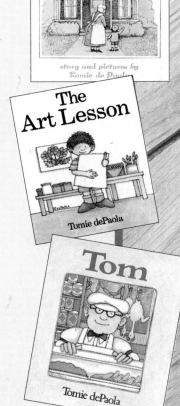

**B**obby was named after his best friend, his grandfather, Bob. When Bobby was just a baby, his grandfather told everyone, "Bobby will be three years old before he can say Grandpa, so I'm going to have him call me Bob."

And "Bob" was the first word Bobby said.

Bob was the one who helped Bobby learn to walk.

"Hold on to my hands, Bobby," his grandfather said. "Now one foot, now the other."

One of the best things Bob and Bobby did was to play with the old wooden blocks that were kept on a shelf, in the small sewing room under the front stairs.

The blocks had letters on two sides, numbers on two sides and pictures of animals and other things on the last two sides. Bob and Bobby would slowly, very slowly put the blocks one on top of the other, building a tall tower. There were thirty blocks.

Sometimes the tower would fall down when only half the blocks were piled up.

Sometimes the tower would be almost finished.

"Just one more block," Bob would say.

"And that's the elephant block," Bobby would say.

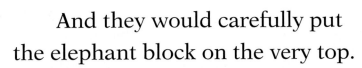

And they would carefully put
the elephant block on the very top.

But Bob would sneeze and the tower would fall
down. Bobby would laugh and laugh.

"Elephants always make you sneeze, Bob,"
Bobby would say.

"We'll just have to try the next time," his
grandfather would say.

Then Bob would sit Bobby on his knee and tell him stories.

"Bob, tell me the story about how you taught me to walk," Bobby would say.

And his grandfather would tell Bobby how he held Bobby's hands and said, "Now one foot, now the other. And before you knew it . . . "

On Bobby's fifth birthday, Bob and he had a special day. They went to the amusement park. They rode a roller coaster, ate hot dogs and ice cream. They had their pictures taken in a machine, and they sang a song and made a phonograph record. And when it got dark, they watched the fireworks.

On the way home, Bob told Bobby stories.

"Now, tell me the story about how you taught me to walk," Bobby said.

And Bob did.

Not long after Bobby's birthday, his grandfather got very sick. Bobby came home and his grandfather wasn't there.

"Bob is in the hospital," Dad told Bobby. "He's had what is called a *stroke*."

"I want to go see him," Bobby said.

"You can't, honey," Mom told him. "Right now Bob's too sick to see anyone. He can't move his arms and legs, and he can't talk. The doctor's not sure if he knows who anyone is. We'll just have to wait and hope Bob gets better."

Bobby didn't know what to do. He didn't want
to eat; he had a hard time going to sleep at night.
Bob just *had* to get better.

Months and months and months went by.
Bob was still in the hospital. Bobby missed his
grandfather.

One day when Bobby came home from school, his father told him that Bob was coming home.

"Now, Bobby," Dad said, "Bob is still very sick. He can't move or talk. When he sees your mother and me, he still doesn't know who we are, and the doctor doesn't think he'll get any better. So, don't be scared if he doesn't remember you."

But Bobby *was* scared. His grandfather *didn't*
remember him. He just lay in bed. And when Dad
carried him, Bob sat in a chair. But he didn't talk
or even move.

One day, Bob tried to
say something to Bobby,
but the sound that came
out was awful. Bobby ran
out of the room.

"Bob sounded like
a monster!" Bobby
cried.

"He can't help it,
Bobby," Mom said.

So, Bobby went back to the room where Bob was sitting.  It looked like a tear was coming down Bob's face.

"I didn't mean to run away, Bob.  I was scared.  I'm sorry," Bobby said.  "Do you know who I am?"

Bobby thought he saw Bob blink his eye.

"Mom, Mom," Bobby called.  "Bob knows who I am."

"Oh, Bobby," Mom said.  "You're just going to upset yourself.  Your grandfather doesn't recognize any of us."

But Bobby knew better.  He ran to the small
sewing room, under the front stairs.  He took the
blocks off the shelf and ran back to where Bob
was sitting.

Bob's mouth made a small smile.

Bobby began to build the tower.

Halfway . . .
Almost to the top . . .
Only one block left.
"OK, Bob," said
Bobby. "Now the
elephant block." And
Bob made a strange
noise that sounded
like a sneeze.

The blocks fell down
and Bob smiled and
moved his fingers up
and down.

Bobby laughed and
laughed. Now he knew
that Bob would get better.

And Bob did. Slowly, he began to talk a little. It sounded strange but he could say "Bobby" just as clear as day. Bob began to move his fingers and then his hands. Bobby still helped to feed his grandfather, but one day Bob could almost hold a spoon by himself. But, he still couldn't walk.

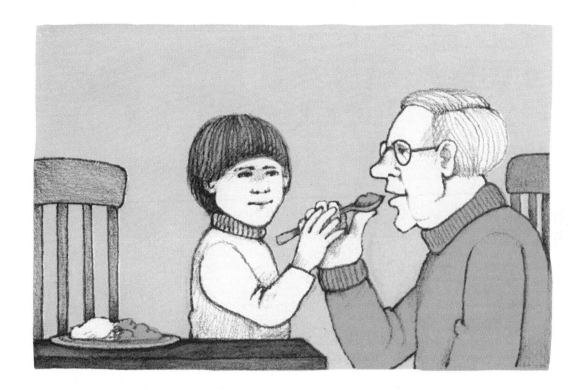

When the weather got nice and warm, Dad carried Bob out to a chair set up on the lawn. Bobby sat with him.

"Bobby," Bob said. "Story." So, Bobby told Bob some stories.

Then, Bob stood up very slowly.

"You.  Me.  Walk," said Bob.

Bobby knew exactly what Bob wanted to do.

Bobby stood in front of Bob and let Bob lean on his shoulders.

"OK, Bob.  Now one foot."

Bob moved one foot.

"Now the other foot."

Bob moved the other.

By the end of the summer, Bob and Bobby could walk to the end of the lawn and Bob could talk better and better each day.

On Bobby's sixth birthday, Bobby got the blocks.  Slowly he built up the tower.  Only one block to go.

"Here, elephant block," Bob said.

Bobby put it on top.

Bob sneezed!

"Elephants always make you sneeze, Bob," Bobby said.  "We'll just have to try the next time. Now, tell me some stories."

Bob did.

Then Bob said, "Bobby, tell story how you teach Bob to walk."

"Well, Bob, you leaned on my shoulders and then I said, 'Now one foot, now the other.' And before you knew it . . ."

# Special Times

Bob and Bobby shared lots of special times together. Think of a special time you spent with someone in your family or with a friend. Choose a way to share your ideas.

- Make a memory box. Put things in your box that remind you of this special time.
- Draw a picture of the special time and tell the class about it. You might tape-record your talk.

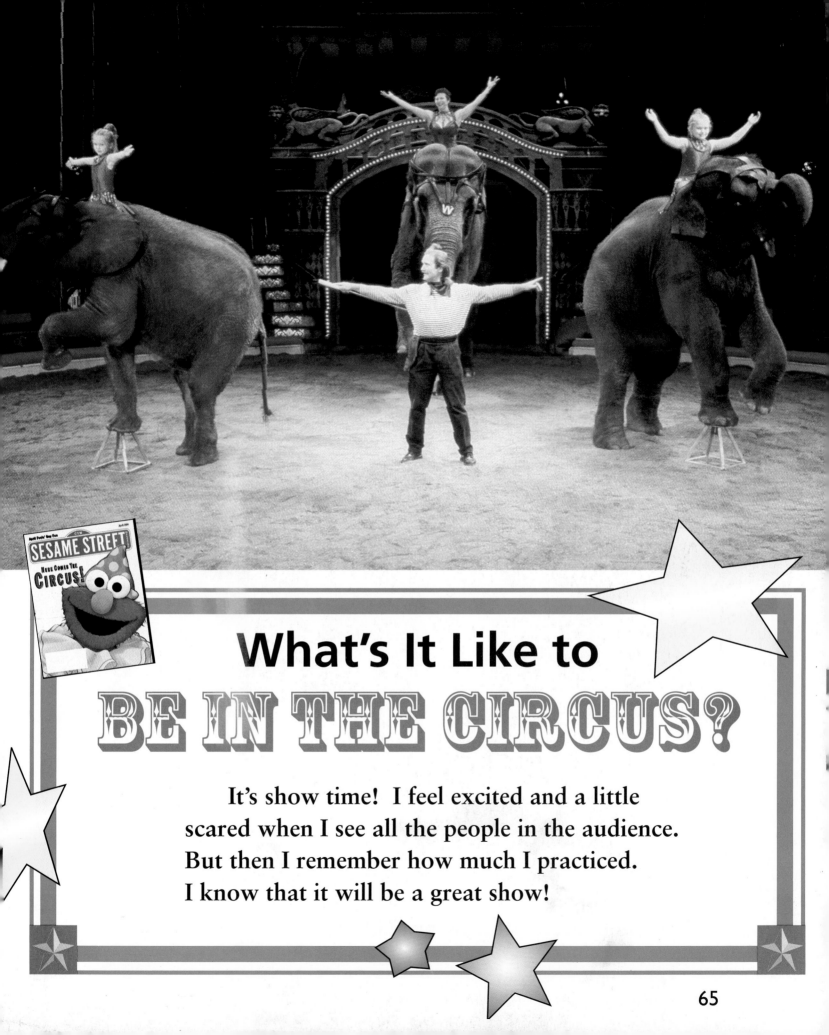

# What's It Like to
# BE IN THE CIRCUS?

It's show time! I feel excited and a little
scared when I see all the people in the audience.
But then I remember how much I practiced.
I know that it will be a great show!

Hi! I'm Skye. This is my big sister, Stormy. We perform with our parents in the Big Apple Circus.

Mom and Dad teach us new tricks. The tricks we perform aren't easy. We have to practice over and over until we get them just right.

When Stormy and I are working, we don't have time to go to school. So our mom teaches us at home in our trailer. She's teaching me the letters that spell my name.

We play and have fun, too. Stormy and I play tag with the other kids whose parents work in the circus. Stormy likes to play chess with Dad, too.

Before the show, Dad gets the elephants, Anna May, Ned, and Amy, ready. Mom helps us get dressed.

# My Family

My mom is by the table, beading a belt.

My dad is sitting, watching the television.

My two brothers are playing basketball outside.

My oldest sister is out on a date.

My second-oldest sister is reading a book.

My little sister is out visiting our cousins.

I'm asleep on the couch!

I'm able to sleep

because I know my family is all around me.

*by Delia Spotted Bear*

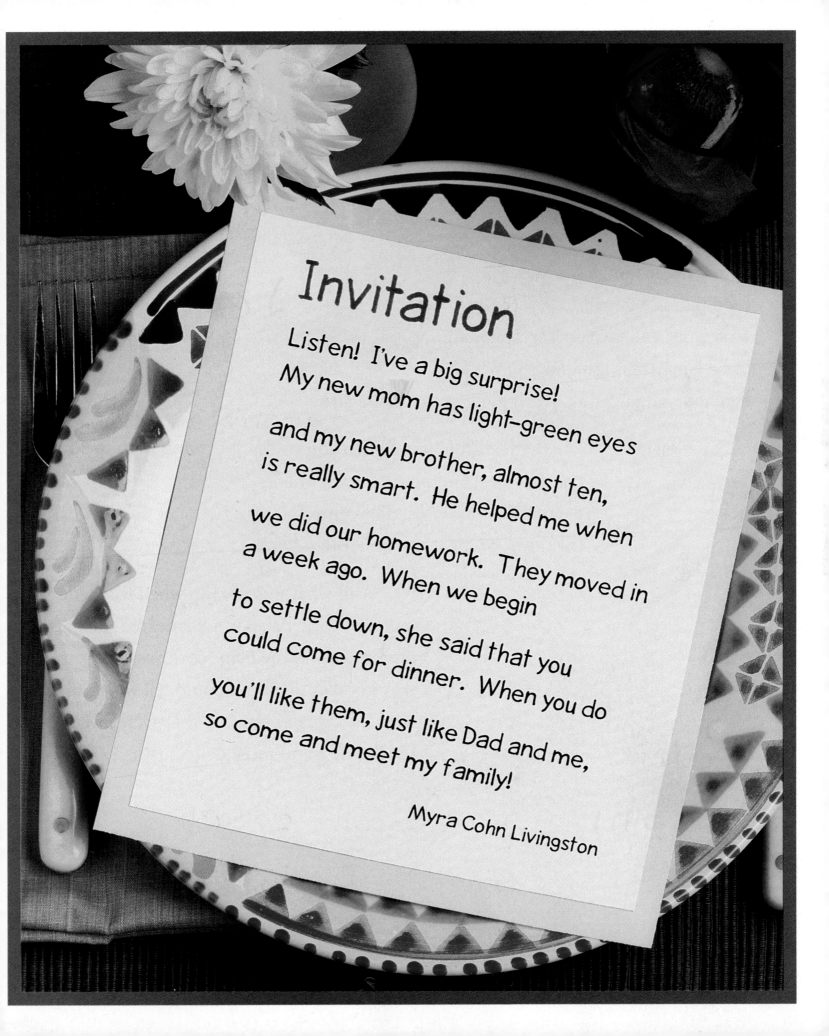

# Invitation

Listen! I've a big surprise!
My new mom has light-green eyes

and my new brother, almost ten,
is really smart. He helped me when

we did our homework. They moved in
a week ago. When we begin

to settle down, she said that you
could come for dinner. When you do

you'll like them, just like Dad and me,
so come and meet my family!

Myra Cohn Livingston

# Meet
# Gary Soto

When I was a boy, my family made tamales, a Mexican food that is difficult to describe with words. A tamale is wrapped up, like a Christmas gift. Sometimes a neighbor might bring over a plate of them as a gift.

Gary, Carolyn, and Mariko Soto

Unlike an onion, which you could peel and peel and never get anywhere, a tamale has a center. The center is the *carne,* or meat, which is often pork.

And what was my job when we made tamales? Using a spoon, I smeared the *masa* (cornmeal) on the *hoja* (cornhusk). I was very good at this. You could tell which ones were my tamales because they were always the heaviest and most delicious!

70

# Meet Ed Martinez

Ed Martinez did not look at pictures of tamales to get an idea of how to draw the illustrations for *Too Many Tamales*. In his own kitchen, he and his wife, Debbi, made their own tamales. They made two batches of tamales to fill the platter that is shown in the story.

73

Snow drifted through the streets and now that it
was dusk, Christmas trees glittered in the windows.

Maria moved her nose off the glass and came back to the counter. She was acting grown-up now, helping her mother make tamales. Their hands were sticky with *masa*. "That's very good," her mother said.

Maria happily kneaded the *masa*. She felt grown-up, wearing her mother's apron. Her mom had even let her wear lipstick and perfume. If only I could wear Mom's ring, she thought to herself.

Maria's mother had placed her diamond ring on the kitchen counter. Maria loved that ring. She loved how it sparkled, like their Christmas tree lights.

When her mother left the kitchen to answer the telephone, Maria couldn't help herself. She wiped her hands on the apron and looked back at the door.

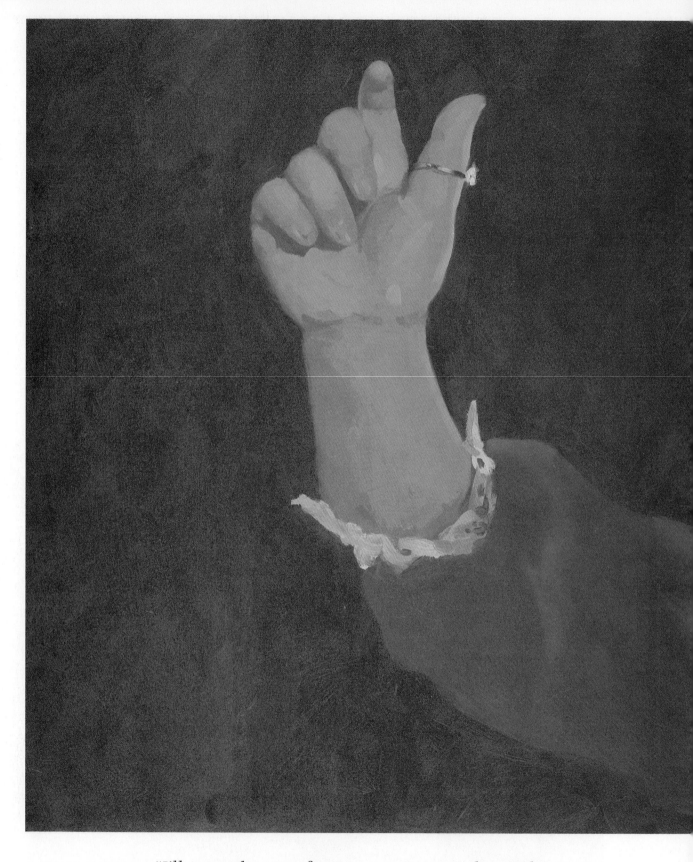

"I'll wear the ring for just a minute," she said
to herself.

The ring sparkled on her thumb.

Maria returned to kneading the *masa*, her hands
pumping up and down. On her thumb the ring
disappeared, then reappeared in the sticky glob of dough.

Her mother returned and took the bowl from her.
"Go get your father for this part," she said.

Then the three of them began to spread *masa* onto corn husks. Maria's father helped by plopping a spoonful of meat in the center and folding the husk. He then placed them in a large pot on the stove.

They made twenty-four tamales as the windows grew white with delicious-smelling curls of steam.

A few hours later the family came over with armfuls of
bright presents: her grandparents, her uncle and aunt, and
her cousins Dolores, Teresa, and Danny.

Maria kissed everyone hello. Then she grabbed
Dolores by the arm and took her upstairs to play, with the
other cousins tagging along after them.

They cut out pictures from the newspaper, pictures of toys they were hoping were wrapped and sitting underneath the Christmas tree. As Maria was snipping out a picture of a pearl necklace, a shock spread through her body.

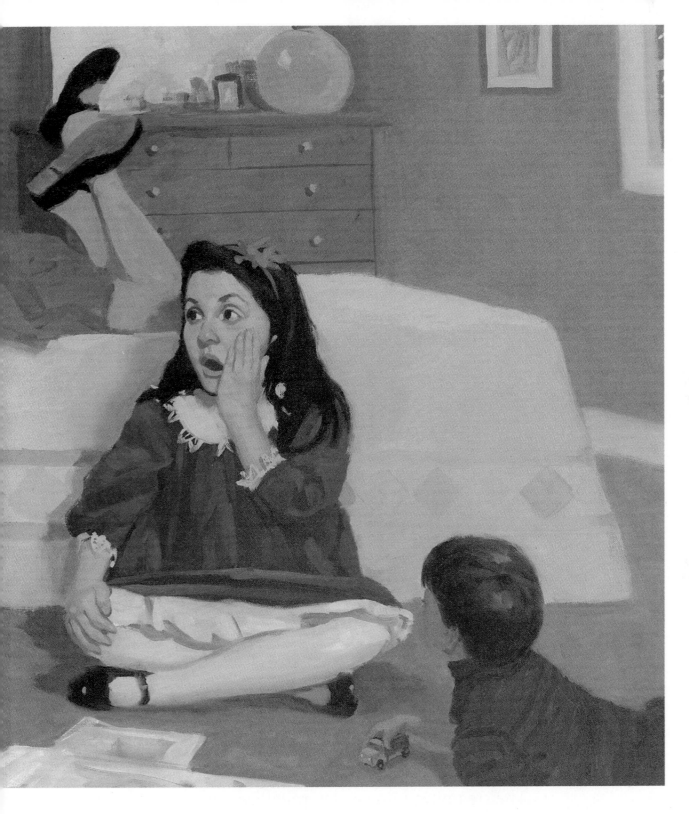

"The ring!" she screamed.

Everyone stared at her. "What ring?" Dolores asked.

Without answering, Maria ran to the kitchen.

The steaming tamales lay piled on a platter.  The ring
is inside one of the tamales, she thought to herself.  It must
have come off when I was kneading the *masa*.

Dolores, Teresa, and Danny skidded into the kitchen
behind her.

"Help me!" Maria cried.

They looked at each other. Danny piped up first.
"What do you want us to do?"

"Eat them," she said. "If you bite something
hard, tell me."

The four of them started eating. They ripped off the husks and bit into them. The first one was good, the second one pretty good, but by the third tamale, they were tired of the taste.

"Keep eating," Maria scolded.

Corn husks littered the floor. Their stomachs were stretched till they hurt, but the cousins kept eating until only one tamale remained on the plate.

"This must be it," she said. "The ring must be in that one! We'll each take a bite. You first, Danny."

Danny was the youngest, so he didn't argue. He took a bite. Nothing.

Dolores took a bite.  Nothing.  Teresa took a big bite.
Still nothing. It was Maria's turn.  She took a deep breath
and slowly, gently, bit into the last mouthful of tamale.

Nothing!

"Didn't any of you bite something hard?" Maria asked.

Danny frowned. "I think I swallowed something hard," he said.

"Swallowed it!" Maria cried, her eyes big with worry. She looked inside his mouth.

Teresa said, "I didn't bite into anything hard, but I think I'm sick." She held her stomach with both hands. Maria didn't dare look into Teresa's mouth!

She wanted to throw herself onto the floor and cry. The ring was now in her cousin's throat, or worse, his belly. How in the world could she tell her mother?

But I have to, she thought.

She could feel tears pressing to get out as she walked
into the living room where the grown-ups sat talking.

They chattered so loudly that Maria didn't know how
to interrupt. Finally she tugged on her mother's sleeve.

"What's the matter?" her mother asked.  She took Maria's hand.

"I did something wrong," Maria sobbed.

"What?" her mother asked.

Maria thought about the beautiful ring that was now sitting inside Danny's belly, and got ready to confess.

Then she gasped.  The ring was on her mother's finger, bright as ever.

"The ring!" Maria nearly screamed.

Maria's mother scraped off a flake of dried *masa*. "You were playing with it?" she said, smiling gently.

"I wanted to wear it," Maria said, looking down at the rug.
Then she told them all about how they'd eaten the tamales.

Her mother moved the ring a little on her finger. It winked a
silvery light. Maria looked up and Aunt Rosa winked at her, too.

"Well, it looks like we all have to cook up another
batch of tamales," Rosa said cheerfully.

Maria held her full stomach as everyone filed into the kitchen, joking and laughing. At first she still felt like crying as she kneaded a great bowl of *masa*, next to Aunt Rosa. As she pumped her hands up and down, a leftover tear fell from her eyelashes into the bowl and for just a second rested on her finger, sparkling like a jewel.

Then Rosa nudged her with her elbow and said, "Hey, *niña*, it's not so bad. Everyone knows that the second batch of tamales always tastes better than the first, right?"

When Dolores, Teresa, and Danny heard that from the other side of the room they let off a groan the size of twenty-four tamales.

Then Maria couldn't help herself: She laughed. And pretty soon everyone else was laughing, including her mother. And when Maria put her hands back into the bowl of *masa*, the leftover tear was gone.

# Lost and Found

Maria and her cousins ate all of the tamales trying to find the missing ring. Think like detectives and come up with another way to solve their problem.

Work with a group or a partner. Choose a way to share your ideas.

- Do a funny skit.
- Write the steps you would follow to solve the problem. You might use a computer.

# HOME COOKING

## What You'll Need

**1 apple**

$\frac{1}{2}$ **cup peanut butter**

$\frac{1}{4}$ **cup sunflower seeds**

# APPLE VOLCANOES

These can get totally messy, but the best part is the yummy peanut butter waiting inside, ready to erupt with taste! Try them with other fillings and toppings to make them even more interesting.

104

## What to Do

1. Core the apple with an apple corer. If you don't have that tool, get a grown-up to help you core the apple with a knife.

**1.**

2. Fill the hole of the apple with the peanut butter. A butter knife works well for this.

3. Sprinkle the sunflower seeds on the peanut butter, and let the volcano erupt with taste in your mouth.

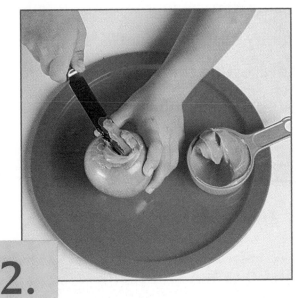

**2.**

**3.**

Makes 1 serving

105

# Pretzels

If you have ever been to New York City, you have probably seen all the pretzel stands on the sidewalks. Now you can make your own pretzels at home, using natural ingredients. It is a lot of fun to make funny shapes, like letters, numbers, people, or other interesting things. Just have fun with the dough and you will surely make great pretzels.

## What You'll Need

1 envelope yeast

$\frac{1}{2}$ cup warm water

1 tablespoon molasses

1 teaspoon salt

$1\frac{1}{2}$ cups whole wheat flour

1 egg, beaten

coarse salt

Yeast

## What to Do

Preheat the oven to 425° F.

1. In a large mixing bowl, dissolve the yeast in the warm water. Add the molasses and salt, and mix well. Stir in the flour.

**1.**

2. Knead the dough with clean hands to get all the air bubbles out. Roll thin, snake-like pieces of dough on a clean counter or table. Form shapes from the pieces, and place them on a baking sheet.

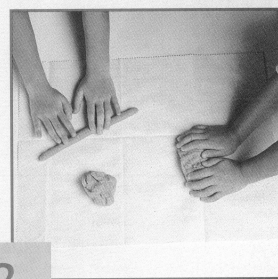

**2.**

3. Brush a little of the beaten egg onto the shapes, and sprinkle them with coarse salt. Place them in the oven for about 10 minutes.

**3.**

Makes 6 – 8 servings

# Seeing Double

Twinsburg, Ohio, is the only place in the world named for twins. Each August thousands of twins gather there for the largest meeting of twins in the world, the Twins Days Festival.

"It's a celebration of being a twin," says Andy Miller, president of the festival committee. "It's a chance for twins to get together, share stories, and meet new friends from around the world."

Twins of all ages, sizes, and nationalities come together for a giant group picture.

▲▲ Twins Kelly and Courtney Friedman, age 13, of Richmond Heights, Ohio, say, "Our dentist and orthodontist are identical twin brothers!"

◀ Twin watching is fun for Eric and Derrick Hill, age 11, from Detroit, Michigan. "The best part about the festival," says Eric, "was seeing so many other twins."

◀ D'Aiselle and Danielle Albeny, age 6, twins from Cleveland, Ohio, sit behind Micah and Marcus Lloyd, age 8, of Cincinnati, Ohio.

▲▲ **Angela and Dawn Alfonsi, age 8, of Livonia, Michigan,** show twin grins with missing front teeth. "We each lost the same tooth within two weeks of each other," say the girls.

◀ **Samantha and Amanda Broszczuk, age 7, of Parma, Ohio,** look alike from the front and the back. But Amanda wants to be a movie star, and Samantha wants to be a ballerina.

# Twin Facts

## Double Diapers

Twins need twice as many things as one baby. One thing is diapers. In just one month, twin babies will use a whopping 640 diapers.

## No Two Alike

Even the most identical twins are not exactly alike — their fingerprints are different!

## Mirror, Mirror

In a mirror you see an opposite picture of yourself. Some twins are opposites of each other. One may be right-handed and the other left-handed.

# THAT'S INCREDIBLE!

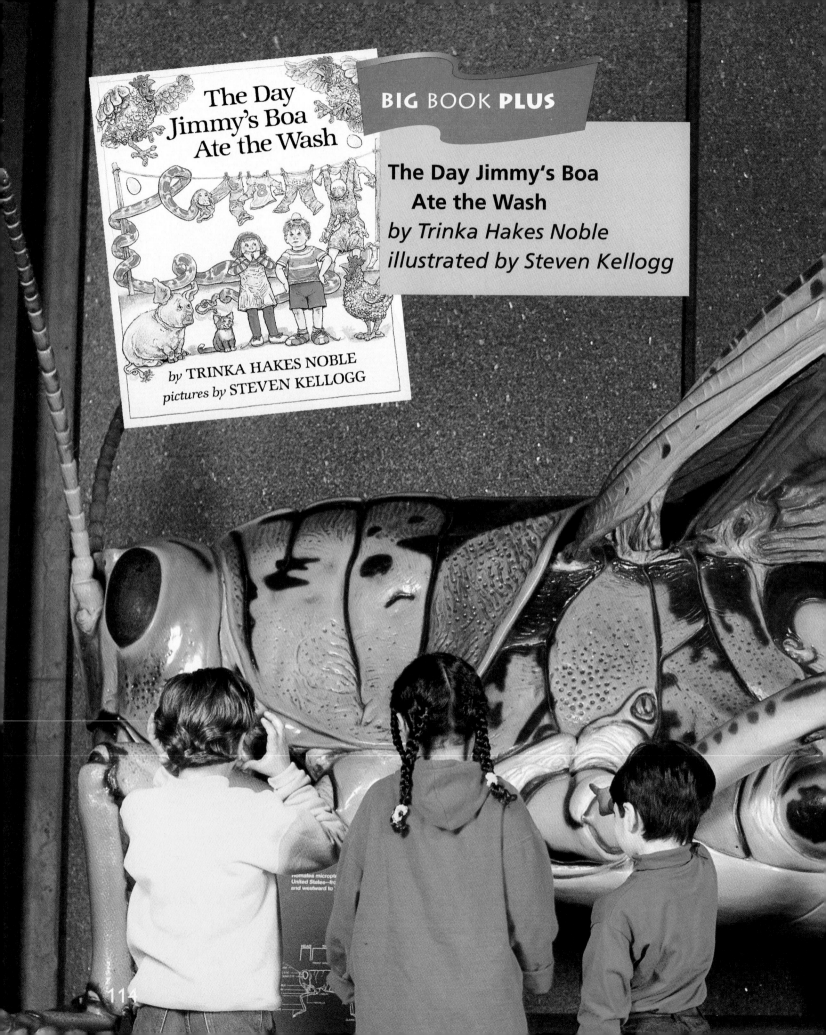

The Day Jimmy's Boa
Ate the Wash
by Trinka Hakes Noble
illustrated by Steven Kellogg

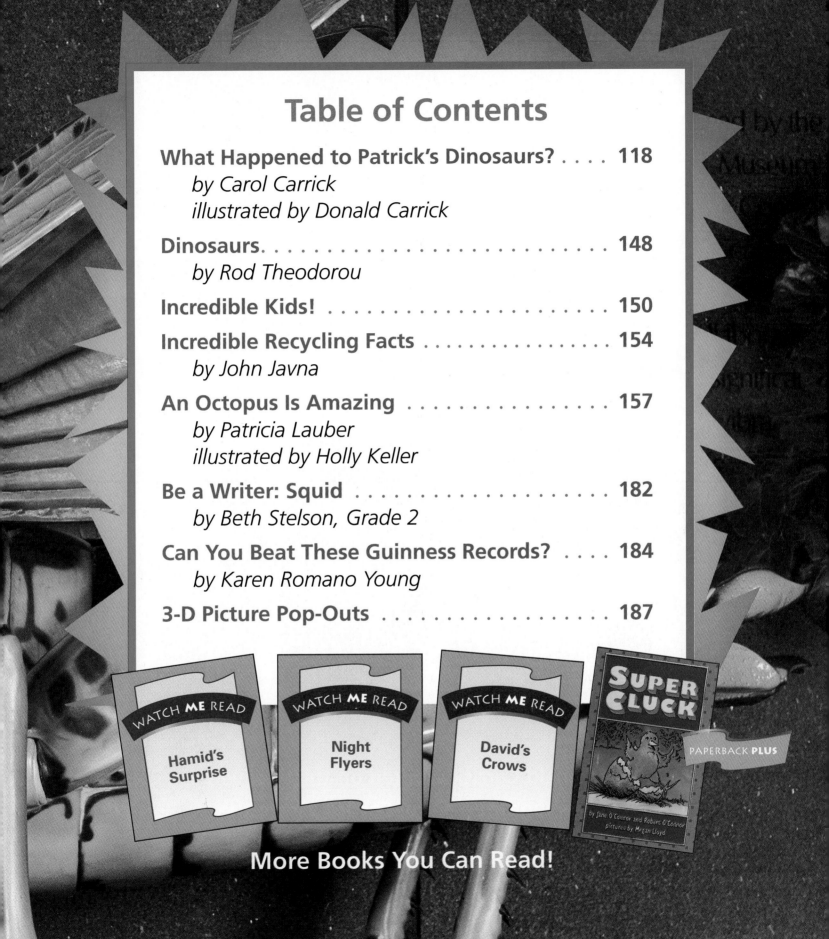

# Table of Contents

WATCH **ME** READ

**Hamid's Surprise**

WATCH **ME** READ

**Night Flyers**

WATCH **ME** READ

**David's Crows**

SUPER CLUCK

PAPERBACK **PLUS**

by Jane O'Connor and Robert O'Connor
pictures by Megan Lloyd

**More Books You Can Read!**

# Meet
# Carol and
# Donald Carrick

**C**arol and Donald Carrick worked on thirty-seven children's books together. Carol Carrick wrote the books, and Donald Carrick illustrated them.

Carol Carrick says, "After *Patrick's Dinosaurs* was such a success, I wanted to write another book about Patrick and his dinosaurs. But I usually have trouble thinking up good ideas. Don suggested doing a book about what made dinosaurs extinct. The idea came to me to tell Patrick's ideas about what happened to the dinosaurs."

Donald Carrick liked to use live animals as models for his illustrations. That was why a crayfish lived in his turkey pan while he worked on *The Pond*, and two turtles lived in the bathtub for *Turtle Pond*. But when he needed dinosaur models, he had to visit museums.

# What Happened to Patrick's Dinosaurs?

by Carol Carrick
Pictures by Donald Carrick

Patrick was helping his big brother, Hank, rake leaves.

119

"Where did they go?" asked Patrick.

"Who?" asked Hank.

"Dinosaurs, of course." Patrick never talked about anything else.

"Well, some people think the world got too hot for dinosaurs," said Hank. "And some think it got too cold. Maybe an asteroid hit the earth and covered it with dust." He showered Patrick with a pile of leaves.

"That's not what *I* think," said Patrick.

"And what do you think?" asked his brother.

"I think that, once upon a time, dinosaurs and people were friends," said Patrick.

"There weren't any people then," said Hank. "Cave men came much later."

"The people didn't live in caves," said Patrick.
"Dinosaurs built them cozy houses."

"I suppose there were dinosaur houses, too," said
Hank.

"That's silly," said Patrick. "Dinosaurs didn't live
in houses. They just made them."

Hank smiled. "What happened when the
dinosaurs got hungry?" he asked.

"They knocked down trees and planted bananas," said Patrick. "And they always shared. Can I have a bite?"

127

"Then dinosaurs invented cars," said Patrick, "because people couldn't run as fast as they could."

"Dinosaurs made cars?" said Hank. "Why not airplanes?"

"They did make airplanes," said Patrick.

"And they made roads for people to drive on."

"Dinosaurs were big and strong so they did all the work."

"If they did everything, what were the people doing all this time?" asked Hank.

"Oh, they got very bored," said Patrick. "So dinosaurs put on shows to make them happy. Some of the smart people learned to do tricks."

"Dinosaurs taught *people* tricks?"

WALTZING TRICERATOPS

2
SHOWS
DAILY

"Dinosaurs wanted to teach people how everything works," explained Patrick. "But people were only interested in recess and lunch."

Hank lay down on a pile of leaves. Patrick lay down, too.

"Guess what happened then," Patrick said.

"I give up."

"Dinosaurs got tired of doing all the work," said Patrick. "And nobody would help them. So they built a big spaceship and left."

"Dinosaurs couldn't fit in a spaceship," said Hank.

"Then how could they leave?" asked Patrick.

"I didn't say they left," Hank said.

"But they did," said Patrick. "And they never came back."

"After a while people forgot that there ever were dinosaurs. They had to take care of themselves now, and they didn't know how."

It grew dark and the first stars came out. Hank and Patrick watched as one bright star moved across the sky.

"You really think dinosaurs are out there?" asked Hank.

Patrick nodded. "But they miss us," he said. "And every so often they check to see how we're doing."

# Where Did They Go?

In the story, Patrick told us what he thought happened to the dinosaurs. What do you think happened? Choose a way to share your ideas.

- Write your own story about the dinosaurs and draw some pictures. Put your story and drawings on large paper to make a dinosaur Big Book.
- Make dinosaur puppets and put on a puppet play. Work with a group or a partner.

# Dinosaurs

*by Rod Theodorou*

## Which was the **biggest** dinosaur?

Brachiosaurus was gigantic. If it were alive today, it would be able to peer over the top of a four-story building. It was so big that you would have needed to stretch up to touch its knee. And scientists have discovered bones of a long-necked dinosaur called Seismosaurus that was even bigger!

Here's how these three dinosaur giants compare with today's heaviest land animal, the African elephant.

**Apatosaurus**

70 feet (21 meters) long
30 tons

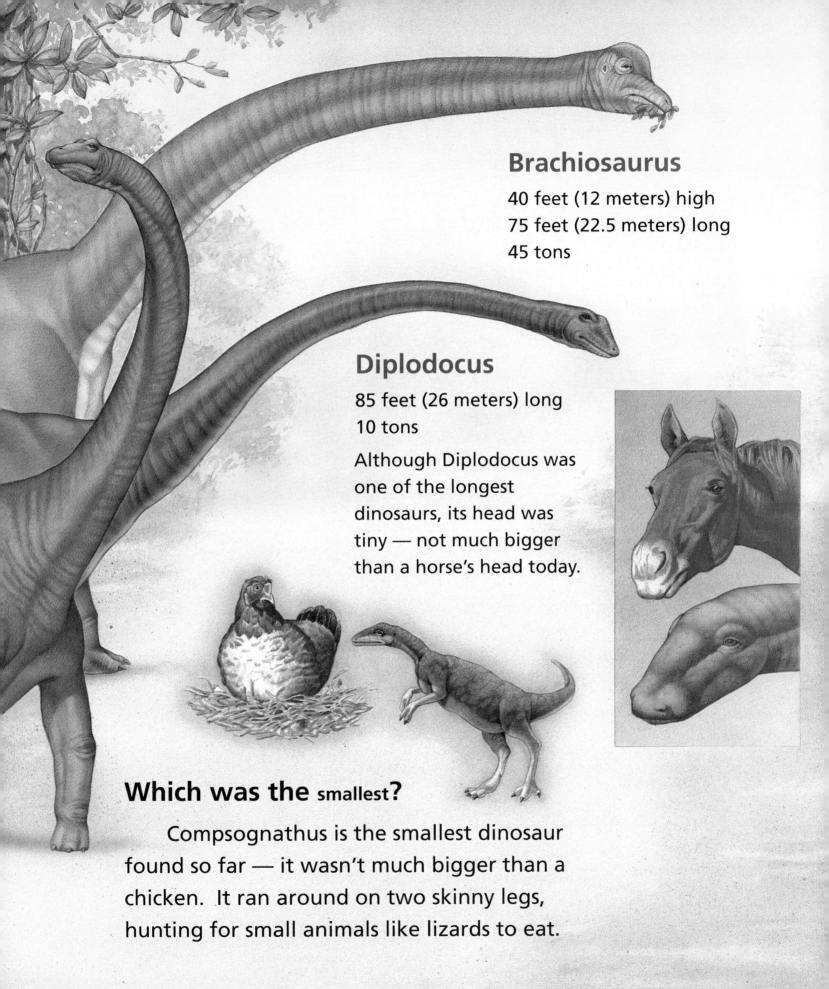

## Brachiosaurus

40 feet (12 meters) high
75 feet (22.5 meters) long
45 tons

## Diplodocus

85 feet (26 meters) long
10 tons

Although Diplodocus was one of the longest dinosaurs, its head was tiny — not much bigger than a horse's head today.

## Which was the smallest?

Compsognathus is the smallest dinosaur found so far — it wasn't much bigger than a chicken. It ran around on two skinny legs, hunting for small animals like lizards to eat.

# ★Incredible Kids!

## Play Ball! Joshua Raiford, 9

Like a lot of kids his age, Joshua Raiford wanted to play baseball. But Harlem, the part of New York City where he lives, had no league. "I asked my mom to start a Little League," says Joshua. "She agreed, if I would practice the piano more." Josh kept his part of the bargain, and his mom kept hers. It took about a year for Josh and his parents to get a league started. Playing fields had to be cleaned up, sponsors found, and teams organized. Finally Josh got his wish – a slot on a team.

# Amazing Grace

Jenny Sikora, 9

**A**lready a pro, Jenny Sikora has been performing for four years with the Cleveland Ballet Dancing Wheels in Cleveland, Ohio. At right, she rehearses a lift with dancer Sabatino Verlezza. He swoops her onto his shoulder from her wheelchair.

Born with a back disorder, Jenny needs braces or a wheelchair. But that's not unusual in the Dancing Wheels ballet company. It welcomes dancers with and without disabilities.

Her mom says Dancing Wheels makes Jenny feel great and that performing has inspired her to want to teach other kids to dance. What does Jenny herself want to be? "A dancer, of course," she says.

# Uplifting Story

John Dow, 10

"**I** don't usually walk my dog, but that day I felt like getting outside," says John Dow of Vienna, Virginia. He's recalling the day when he walked into the path of an emergency. His neighbor, in the background here, was on a riding mower. It hit a tree and flipped over, pinning her underneath. "I heard her call, 'Help!'" says John. "I wasn't scared. I ran over and lifted the mower about 8 inches off the ground" — high enough for the woman to roll to safety. How did a 72-pound boy lift a 400-pound mower? John's not sure. For bravery beyond his years, John was named Vienna Citizen of the Year.

# Safety First

Ursula Sawyer, 10

**B**y the time Ursula Sawyer reached her tenth birthday, she had already saved 12 lives. Earlier this year, the Washington, D.C., third-grader woke up just before dawn to discover that a fire had broken out in the bedroom she shared with her younger sister Sheena. The flames were blocking their way out. "I didn't have time to be scared," Ursula says. "The fire was rising, so I got my sister's hand, and we jumped over it." Ursula immediately woke up 11 other family members in the house and phoned 911. Later the fire fighters made Ursula an honorary fire chief.

# INCREDIBLE RECYCLING FACTS
## Take a Guess...

*by John Javna*

## STAMP OUT STYROFOAM

If you lined up all the Styrofoam cups made in just one day, how far would they reach?

**A)** A mile **B)** Around the Earth **C)** Across the U.S.

Answer: B. Incredible! They would circle the entire planet . . . and reach a little further, too!

## SHOWER POWER

About how many milk cartons can you fill with the water from a five-minute shower?

**A)** 5 **B)** 15 **C)** 50

Answer: C. Think how high 50 milk cartons stacked on top of one another would reach!

## BE A PAPER-SAVER

If you stacked up all the paper an average
American uses in a year, the pile would be as tall as . . .

**A)** A two-story house    **B)** An elephant's eye    **C)** A car

Answer: A. Believe it or not, as high as a two-story house!

## PRESTO, ON! . . . PRESTO, OFF!

You can save up to 20,000 gallons of water a year
by not letting the water run. That's enough to fill:

**A)** A garbage can    **B)** A big truck    **C)** A swimming pool

Answer: C. You can save enough water to fill a swimming pool.

## Meet Patricia Lauber

Patricia Lauber writes both fiction and nonfiction books. She writes about anything that interests her — life in other countries, sea animals, dogs, forests, horses. Patricia Lauber met the horse in this photograph when she was getting information for a book about ranching.

**Ms. Lauber with Buster**

## Meet Holly Keller

When Holly Keller was a child, she remembers spending hours copying all of the birds from a bird book. Then she drew lots of horses. Now she writes and illustrates her own books, and sometimes she does illustrations for other authors.

**Holly Keller is interested in all kinds of sea animals. She loved feeding this dolphin!**

This Is a Let's-Read-and-Find-Out Science Book®

# AN OCTOPUS IS AMAZING

by Patricia Lauber • illustrated by Holly Keller

# THERE ARE MORE THAN 150 KNOWN KINDS OF OCTOPUSES

**GIANT OCTOPUS**
Length: up to 17 feet
Weight: up to 110 pounds
Found in temperate waters of
the northern Pacific, from
California to Japan.

**COMMON OCTOPUS**
Length: up to 30 inches
Weight: from 2 to 3 pounds
Found all over the world in
tropical to temperate waters.

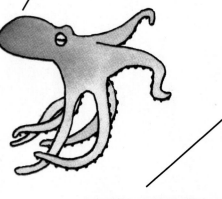

**BLUE-RINGED OCTOPUS**
Length: from $1\frac{1}{2}$ to 4 inches
Weight: from 2 to 3 ounces
Found in tropical waters near Australia
and Indonesia. It is the only octopus
whose bite is poisonous to humans.

**DWARF OCTOPUS**
Length: 4 inches
Weight: $\frac{1}{2}$ ounce
Found in Caribbean waters, this
tiny octopus is a popular choice for
home aquariums.

### How to Measure an Octopus

Measure length from tip of bag
to tip of arm.

An octopus is an animal that lives in the sea. It has
a soft, bag-shaped body and eight rubbery arms.

The common octopus lives in a den near shore.
It may make its den in a cave or a wrecked ship,
in a shell or a tin can, under a rock or in a crack in
a rock.

Every octopus lives alone. Its den is small, just
big enough to hold the octopus. An octopus can
squeeze into a small space because it has no
backbone. In fact, it has no bones at all.

An octopus can change color in a flash.

Usually the octopus matches its surroundings and is hard to see. If it climbs into an empty shell, it turns pink and gray. If it crawls among rocks and seaweeds, it may turn brown and gray and green.

An octopus can have colored spots or stripes. It can be half one color and half another.

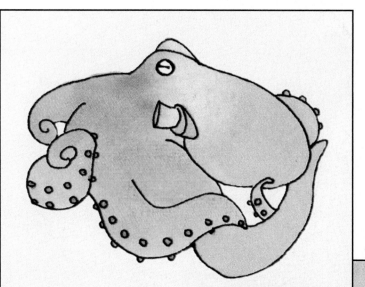

Color changes help an octopus to hide or to escape
from enemies. They may also show how an octopus is
feeling. Scientists say an angry octopus turns dark red.
A frightened one turns pale. An octopus that is
enjoying a meal shows pleasure by changing color.

An octopus has a big appetite. Crabs are its favorite food, but it also likes lobsters, clams, and other shellfish.

Sometimes an octopus waits in its den until a meal passes by. Then it reaches out an arm and grabs.

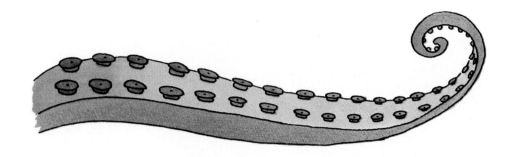

Each arm is lined with suckers. They work like little rubber suction cups. The common octopus has 240 suckers on each arm.

The octopus holds its food with its suckers and examines it.

The octopus carries its catch toward its mouth. The mouth is on the underside of the body, and inside it is a hard, curved beak. The octopus uses its beak to crack the shell of its prey. It squirts the prey with poison from a gland in its mouth. When the prey is paralyzed or dead, the octopus feeds.

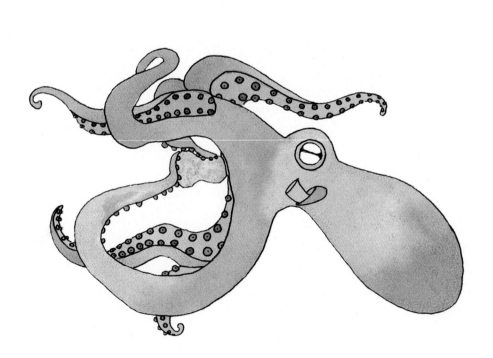

**MOUTH**

Sometimes an octopus leaves its den and hunts for food. It hunts by sight, using its sharp eyes.

The octopus may crawl along, using its suckers to hold on to rocks and pulling itself forward.

Or it may jet, by drawing in water and shooting it out through a tube, which is called the siphon. With each spurt, the octopus jets through the sea.

Once the octopus spies something to eat, it spreads its webbed arms. It floats down and wraps itself around its prey. It may store crabs or clams in its suckers and take them home to eat.

When an octopus has eaten, it tidies up its den.
It clears out the shells, using its siphon to blow them
away.

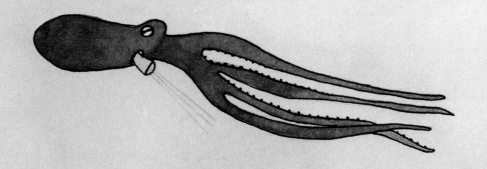

Sometimes other animals try to eat an octopus. The octopus does not fight. Instead, it tries to hide or escape.

If a big fish attacks, the octopus changes colors and jets off. The octopus no longer looks like the animal the fish was going to attack. And so the fish is fooled.

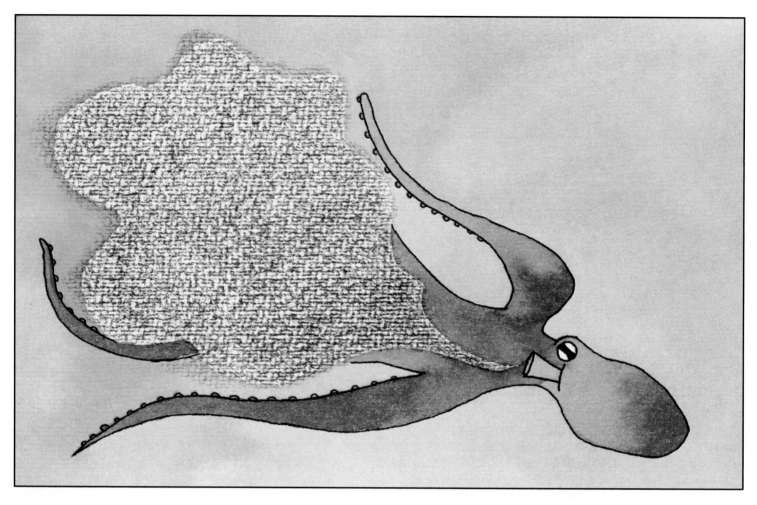

An octopus can also give off an ink-black liquid through its siphon. The ink forms a blob that has the shape and smell of an octopus. The enemy attacks the blob. The octopus, which has turned black, escapes.

That is how an octopus defends itself against
the moray eel, one of its most dangerous enemies.
A moray eel is big enough to swallow an octopus
whole. It has sharp teeth and a keen sense of
smell, which it uses in hunting.

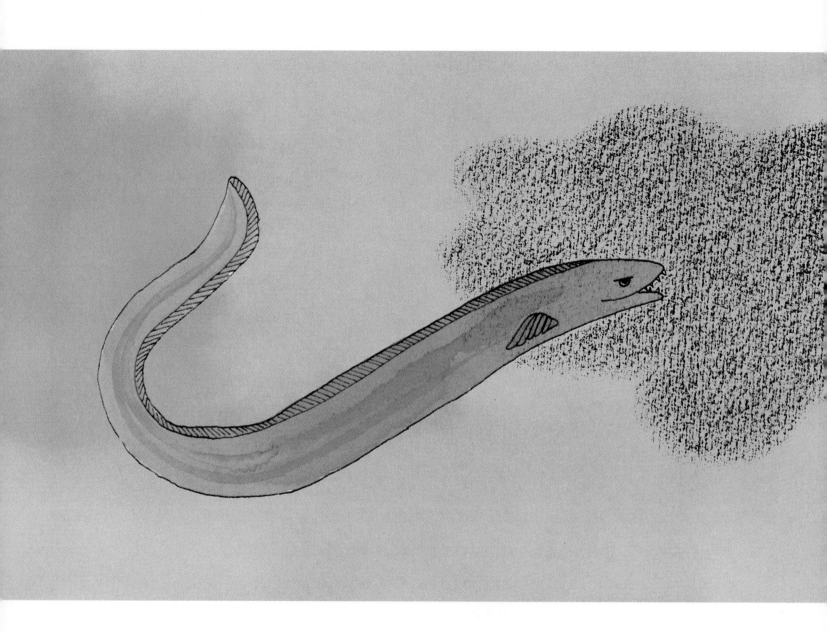

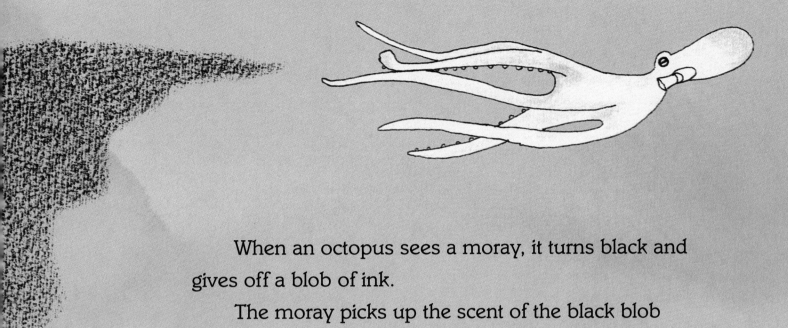

When an octopus sees a moray, it turns black and gives off a blob of ink.

The moray picks up the scent of the black blob and attacks it. The octopus turns white and jets away.

Sometimes a moray eel is able to tear off one of the octopus's arms before the octopus escapes. If this happens, the octopus can hunt and travel with seven arms. And in time, it grows a new arm.

A female octopus mates when she is one to two years old. A few weeks after mating she finds a den and starts to lay her eggs. A common octopus lays thousands of eggs, more than 100,000. It takes her a week or more to lay them.

Each egg is the size of half a grain of rice and has a stem. The female weaves and glues the stems together, making strings about four inches long. She hangs the strings in her den.

From then on, the female spends all her time taking care of her eggs. She does not hunt or eat.

The eggs take four to six weeks or more to
hatch.  The female guards them from hungry fishes.
She keeps the water around the eggs fresh and
clean by blowing on the strings and running her
arms through them.  When the eggs hatch, the
female's job is done and she dies.

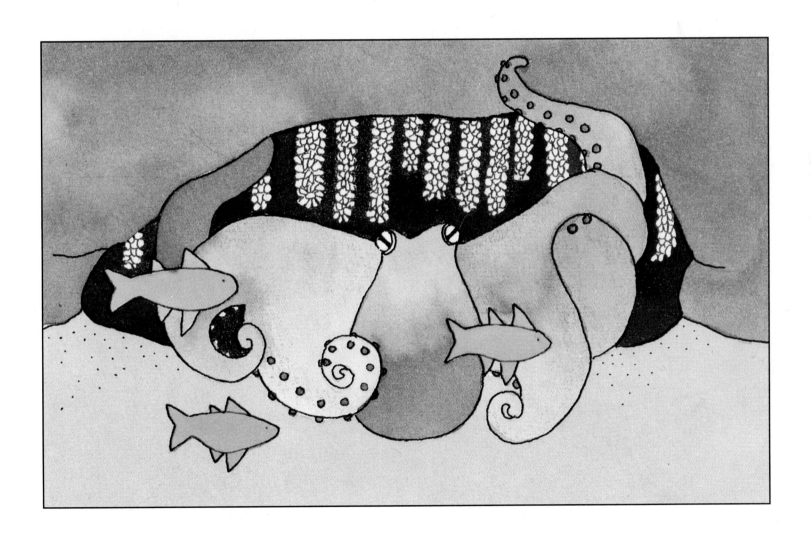

The newly hatched young are tiny, no bigger than fleas. They can change color and give off ink, but they cannot jet or crawl or hide in dens. For a month or more they drift in the sea. Most become food for fishes and other animals. Only a few live to grow up. As they do, they become surprisingly clever animals.

Long ago, people learned that an octopus is good at solving problems. If an octopus cannot open a clam, it waits for the clam to open itself. Then it places a pebble between the two shells. The clam can no longer close up tight, and the octopus eats it.

If an octopus is given a glass jar with a crab inside, it tries to get at the crab. After a few tries, it solves the problem. It takes the top off the jar.

Being able to solve problems is a sign of intelligence.

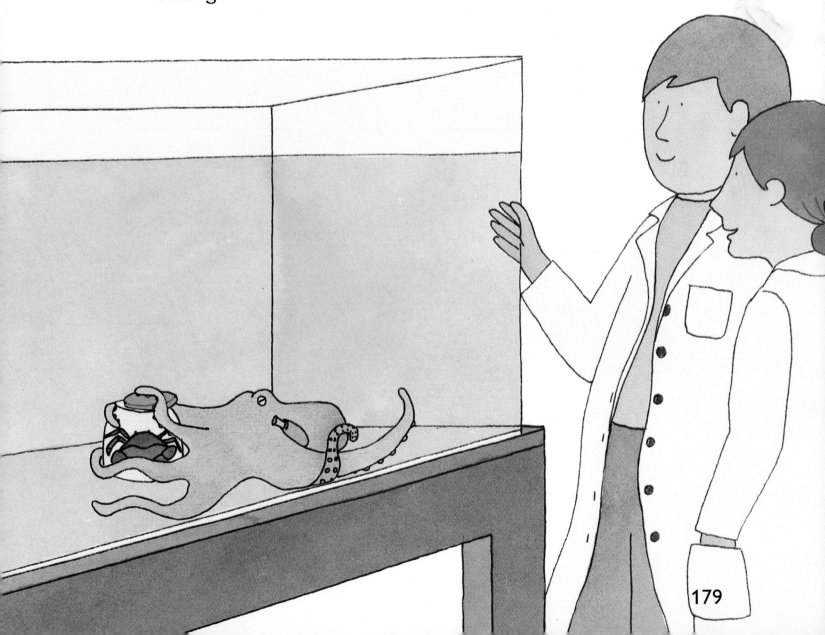

In the wild, octopuses are shy. In aquariums and labs they seem to like the people they get to know. They enjoy being stroked. And they are playful. Playfulness is another sign of intelligence. They play tug-of-war with people. They also play jokes. A person who annoys an octopus may get squirted.

An octopus is truly amazing.

# It's Amazing All Right!

**W**hat is so amazing about an octopus? Think about some of the things you learned in the story. Choose a way to share your ideas.

- Draw an octopus on a large piece of paper. Write an interesting fact on each arm.
- Make a chart. List some facts about the octopus. Use a large sheet of paper or oak tag.

When an octopus loses an arm, it grows a new one.

181

# Squid

## A Report by Beth Stelson

Beth's class was learning about oceans.
She wrote a research report about squid
and found out some amazing things.

### Squid

This is my report on squid. The squid
has a big head with ten arms attached to it.
Two of the arms have long tentacles and
on the tentacles are suction cups. Like
octopuses, squid can change their color to
blend in with their surroundings.

When squid have their babies, they lay
their eggs and put a yucky goo on the eggs.
The mother squid loses her strength and
dies. When squid hatch, they look very tasty
to some creatures, and they will eat them.

Squid can be very different sizes. The
giant squid can be up to seventy feet long.

Squid can mistake humans as their
enemies and kill humans. There is a story

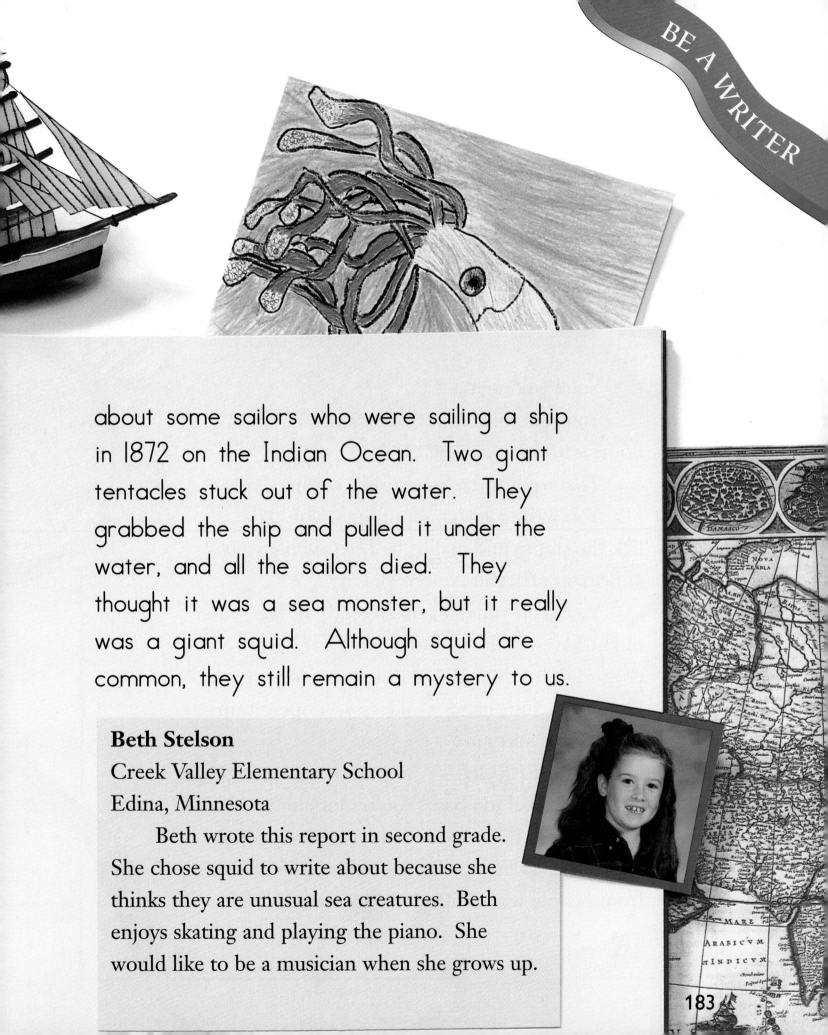

about some sailors who were sailing a ship in 1872 on the Indian Ocean. Two giant tentacles stuck out of the water. They grabbed the ship and pulled it under the water, and all the sailors died. They thought it was a sea monster, but it really was a giant squid. Although squid are common, they still remain a mystery to us.

**Beth Stelson**

Creek Valley Elementary School

Edina, Minnesota

Beth wrote this report in second grade. She chose squid to write about because she thinks they are unusual sea creatures. Beth enjoys skating and playing the piano. She would like to be a musician when she grows up.

183

# Can You Beat These Guinness Records?

*by Karen Romano Young*

You've done it.

You rollerbladed for 52 straight hours without stopping!

That's got to be the world's record.

You write a letter about what you did, lick the stamp and mail it to *The Guinness Book of Records* office in New York City.

You keep your fingers crossed. In fact, you might have set the world's record for keeping fingers crossed. Then, one day, a letter comes back from Guinness. Your hands shake as you open it up.

"We're sorry . . ."

*AAARRRRGH!*

Don't feel too bad. You're not alone. Mark Young, the editor of the American edition of *The Guinness Book of Records*, gets a ton of letters from people who don't make it into the book.

Hundreds are sent from kids. Young feels bad about saying "no" to so many hopefuls.

What's the problem, Mr. Young? Why don't you just say YES?

"One problem is, people try to break records that aren't in the book. If a record isn't in the book, there's a reason," answers Young.

Like what? "Like eating the most hot dogs in one sitting, for instance," says Young. "We took all the eating records out of the book a few years ago. They were just too dangerous." (People sometimes choked on food or got sick.)

So it's a good idea to try to break records that are already in Guinness.

## Records You Can Shoot For

### Skipping Rope

The most nonstop turns of a rope was 14,628.

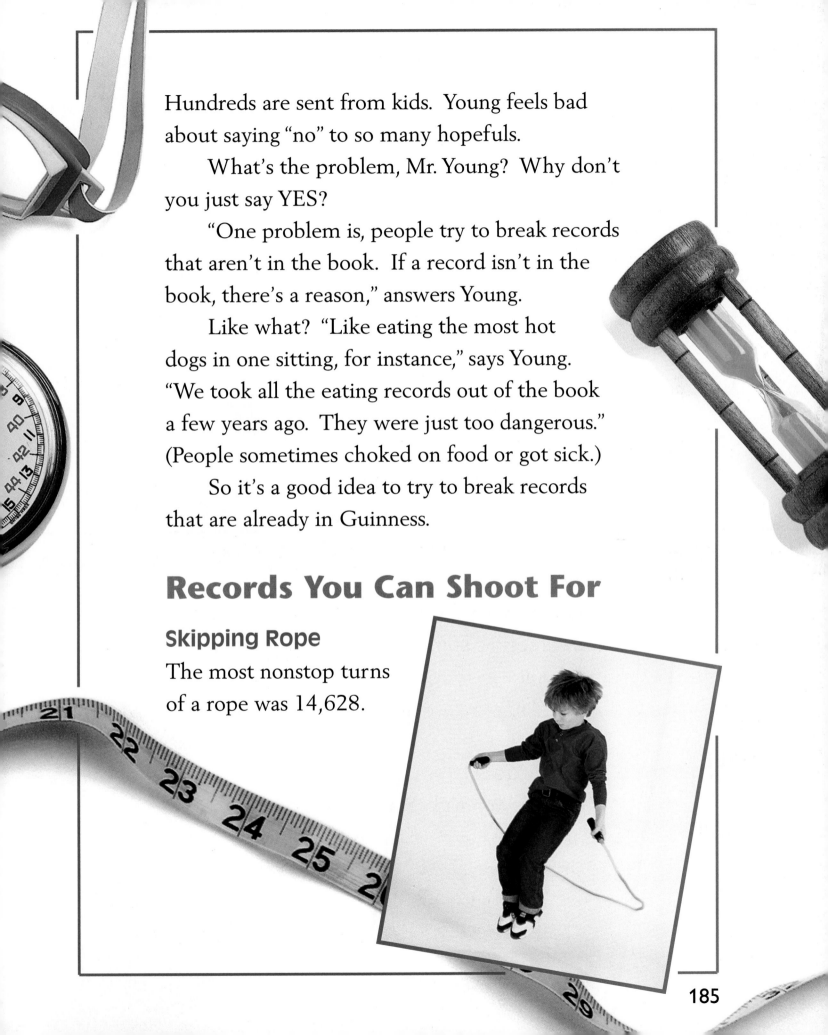

## Balancing on One Foot

The longest time spent on one foot is 55 hours, 35 minutes, 17 seconds.

## Somersaulting

The tops is 8,341 forward rolls (covering a distance of 12 miles, 390 yards) in 10 hours, 30 minutes.

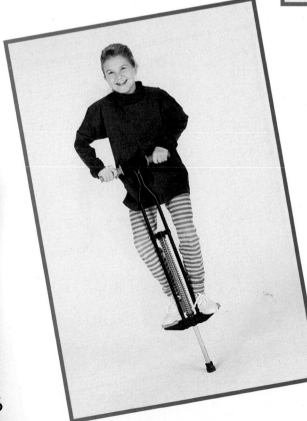

## Pogo-Stick Jumping

The most jumps ever without stopping is 177,737.

# 3-D Picture POP-OUTS

**D**eep inside this picture is a howling wolf standing on top of a hill. On the next page, you may see a toothy alligator coming right toward you.

If you already know how to look at 3-D pictures like these, the animals will pop out at you. If you've never done it before, turn the page to learn the trick.

## About 3-D Pictures

These aren't hidden picture games, where you look for lots of hard-to-find objects all over the page. Instead, you have to look for one big animal to appear in each picture.

When you see an animal, it won't look flat like the photos on these pages. It'll be "3-D," which means it will look a lot like a hologram.

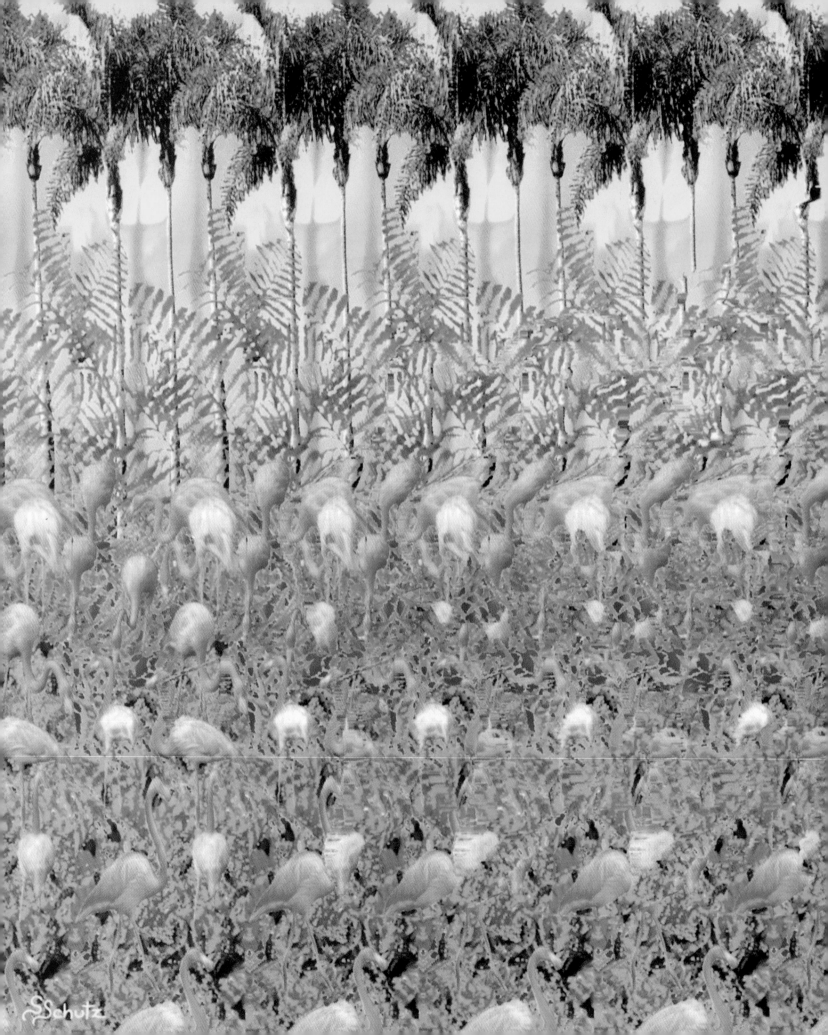

# How to See the Animals

Seeing the animals isn't easy at first, so relax and take your time. It helps if you are in a quiet room with good light. Here's how to make the animals pop out:

1. Hold the picture close to your eyes and stare as if you're looking straight *through* it (the way you would look through a window).

2. *Slowly* move the picture away from your face. *Don't* cross your eyes and *don't* focus them on the picture. Instead, keep pretending to look right through the picture, and let it be fuzzy.

3. When you are holding the book about as far away as you would for reading it, you may start seeing the 3-D animal. Keep staring beyond the picture, and the 3-D picture should appear. Wow! But if you can't see them, don't feel bad — you're not alone!

These drawings show what's hiding in the 3-D pop-out pictures.

**PAGE 187**

**PAGE 188**

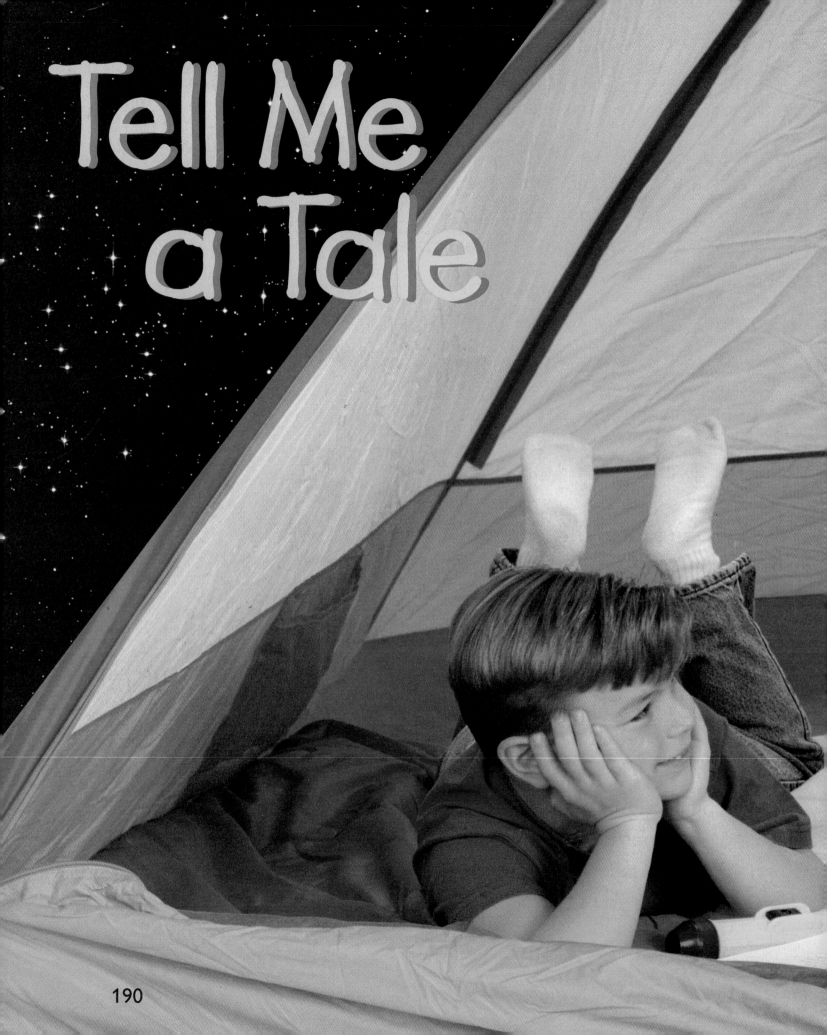

# Tell Me a Tale

**Bringing the Rain to Kapiti Plain**
*by Verna Aardema*
*illustrated by Beatriz Vidal*

# Table of Contents

**WATCH ME READ**

Rain Cloud Island

**WATCH ME READ**

A Friend for King Amadou

**WATCH ME READ**

Maui Hooks Hawaii

The Rooster Who Went to His Uncle's Wedding

PAPERBACK PLUS

**More Books You Can Read!**

# Meet Lily Toy Hong

Lily Toy Hong grew up in a large family of nine children. Even as a young girl, she knew that someday she would write and illustrate children's books.

Through her books, Lily Toy Hong retells stories that were told in China long ago. *Two of Everything* and *How the Ox Star Fell from Heaven*, another book by Lily Toy Hong, are based on Chinese folktales.

# Two of Everything

## Lily Toy Hong

Once long ago, in a humble little hut, lived Mr. Haktak and his wife, Mrs. Haktak. They were old and very poor. What little they ate came from their tiny garden.

In a lucky year when the harvest was plentiful, Mr. Haktak had a little extra to take to the village. There he traded turnips, potatoes, and other vegetables for clothing, lamp oil, and fresh seeds.

One spring morning when Mr. Haktak was digging in his garden, his shovel struck something hard. Puzzled, he dug deeper into the dark ground until he came upon an ancient pot made of brass. "How odd," said Mr. Haktak to himself. "To think that I have been digging here all these years and never came upon this pot before! I will take it home. Maybe Mrs. Haktak can find some use for it."

The pot was big and heavy for old Mr. Haktak. As he stumbled along, his purse, which contained his last five gold coins, fell to the ground. He tossed it into the pot for safekeeping and staggered home.

His wife greeted him at the door. "Dear husband, what a strange pot!" Mr. Haktak explained how he found the pot. "I wonder what we can do with it," said Mrs. Haktak. "It looks too large to cook in and too small to bathe in."

As Mrs. Haktak leaned over to peer into the pot, her hairpin — the only one she owned — fell in. She felt around in the pot, and suddenly her eyes grew round with surprise. "Look!" she shouted. "I've pulled out TWO hairpins, exactly alike, and TWO purses, too!" Sure enough, the purses were identical, and so were the hairpins. Inside each purse were five gold coins!

Mr. Haktak was so excited he jumped up and down. "Let's put my winter coat inside the pot. If we are lucky again the pot will make two coats, and then we will both stay warm." So into the pot went one coat — and out came TWO coats.

They began to search the house and quickly put more things into the magical pot. "If only we had some meat," wished Mr. Haktak, "or fresh fruit, or one delicious sweet cake."

207

Mrs. Haktak smiled. "I know how we can get anything we want," she said. She put their ten coins into one purse, then threw it into the pot. She pulled out two purses with ten coins in each.

"What a clever wife I have!" cried Mr. Haktak. "Each time we do this we will have twice as much money as before!"

The Haktaks worked late into the night, filling and emptying the pot until the floor was covered with coins.

Morning came, and off went Mr. Haktak with a long list of things to buy in the village. Instead of vegetables, his basket was full of gold coins.

Mrs. Haktak finished all of her chores and sat down to enjoy a cup of tea. She sipped her tea and admired the brass pot. Then with a grateful heart, she knelt and embraced it. "Dear pot, I do not know where you came from, but you are my best friend." She stooped over the pot to look inside.

At that very moment, Mr. Haktak returned.  His arms were so full of packages that he had to kick the door open.  Bang!  Mrs. Haktak was so startled that she lost her balance and fell headfirst into the pot!

Mr. Haktak ran over and grabbed his wife's legs.  He pulled and tugged until she slid out onto the floor.  But when he looked at the pot again, he gasped.  Two more legs were sticking straight out of it!  Naturally, he took hold of the ankles and pulled.

Out came a second person!  She looked exactly like his wife.

The new Mrs. Haktak sat silently on the floor looking lost. But the first Mrs. Haktak cried, "I am your one and only wife! Put that woman back into the pot right now!"

Mr. Haktak yelled, "No! If I put her back we will not have two women but THREE. One wife is enough for me!"

He backed away from his angry wife, and tripped and fell headfirst into the pot himself!

Both Mrs. Haktaks rushed to rescue him. Each grasped an ankle, and together they pulled him out. There were two more legs in the pot. So they pulled out the other Mr. Haktak, too.

"Just what use does one Mr. Haktak have for another!" Mr. Haktak cried angrily. "This pot is not as wonderful as we thought it to be. Now even our troubles are beginning to double."

But his wife had been thinking while he was yelling.

"Calm down," she said. "It is good that the other Mrs. Haktak has her own Mr. Haktak. Perhaps we will become best of friends. After all, we are so alike he will be a brother to you and she a sister to me. With our pot we can make two of everything, so there will be plenty to go around."

And that is what they did. The Haktaks built two fine new homes. Each house had identical teapots, rice bowls, silk embroideries, and bamboo furniture.

From the outside the houses looked exactly alike, but there was one difference. Hidden in one house was a big brass pot. Of course, the Haktaks were always very careful not to fall into it again!

The new Haktaks and the old Haktaks did become good friends. The neighbors thought that the Haktaks had grown so rich that they decided to have two of everything — even themselves!

# A Very Different Pot

**I**f you found a pot that gave back two of everything, what would you put in it? Make a pot. Think of one thing that you would like to put into the pot and draw a picture of it. Put your picture in the pot. What happens now that you have two? Make up a funny story and tell it to the class.

# Amor de madre
# (A Mother's Love)

retold by Ramón, Andrea, and Israel Mosqueda

illustrated by Francisco X. Mora

Once upon a time there was a wolf who lived happily with her cub in a beautiful cave high in the mountains. She was very sure that nothing could happen to her cub as long as they were living there. But the cub was a mischievous little rascal. So one day he left the cave while his mother was sleeping. He went out along the paths because he wanted to find out about the place where he was living. And he went without saying a word to his mother. Afterwards, he didn't know how to get home again.

Había una vez una loba que vivía feliz con su cachorro en una hermosa cueva en lo más alto de la sierra. Allí vivía muy confiada de que a su lobito nada le pasaría. Pero el lobito era muy travieso y juguetón. Así que un día se salió de la cueva mientras su madre dormía. Se fue por los caminos, pues quería conocer el lugar donde vivía. Y se fue sin decirle nada a su mamá. Después ya no supo cómo regresar.

His mother couldn't find him when she woke up. She went out to look for him on the slopes, asking everybody she met if he or she had seen him. She met a coyote and asked him anxiously, "Brother coyote, brother coyote, you're always out on the paths. Tell me if you've seen my little cub along your way."

Cuando se despertó, su mamá no lo encontró. Se fue a buscarlo por las laderas, preguntando a cuantos se encontraba por el camino por su hijo. Se encontró con un coyote y ella angustiada le preguntó: —Hermano coyote, hermano coyote, tú que recorres los caminos, dime si por donde tú has pasado has visto a mi hijito.

"Tell me, what does your little cub look like?" asked the coyote.

"Well, I'll tell you," the wolf answered, "I don't like to brag, but my little cub has eyes like a pair of stars, a little mouth red as a pomegranate, pointy little ears, and fur soft and black as velvet. And, of course," the wolf concluded proudly, "he's very healthy and intelligent."

—Dime, ¿cómo es tu hijito? —preguntó el coyote.

—Pues verás —respondió la loba—, no es para presumir, pero mi hijito tiene los ojitos como dos luceros, la boquita es roja y chiquita como la granada, las orejas son paraditas, su pelo es suave y negro como terciopelo. Y, desde luego, es muy robusto e inteligente —terminó de decir la loba muy orgullosa.

The coyote thought for a minute and then said, "Well, then, I guess the cub I just saw down the path a ways must not be yours, because he had sleep in his eyes, a runny nose, droopy ears, and grimy fur; and he was so rickety he could hardly walk . . ."

"Good heavens!" cried the wolf. "That's my baby!"

El coyote pensó un poco y contestó: —Bueno, pues el que acabo de ver por el camino seguramente no era tu hijo, pues tenía los ojos lagañosos, el hocico sucio, las orejas caídas, el pelo roñoso y estaba tan flaco que no se podía estar de pie...

—¡Ay! ¡Ay! —exclamó la loba—. ¡Ése es mi hijo!

The coyote looked surprised. "But I thought you said your cub was beautiful?"

"Hasn't anybody ever told you," replied the wolf, "that no mother thinks her baby is ugly? A mother sees her child through the eyes of love."

And away she went to find her cub.

El coyote, sorprendido, le dijo: —Pues, ¿no dijiste que tu hijo era hermoso?

La loba contestó: —Pues, ¿no sabes tú que para una madre no hay hijo feo, pues lo mira con ojos de amor?

Y la loba se alejó en busca de su pequeño.

# The Rooster and the Beautiful Coat

## A Description by Jennifer Mei

Good descriptions can really make a story come alive!
See if you can picture the rooster's coat
from Jennifer's description.

**Jennifer Mei**
Harvard Kent School
Charlestown, Massachusetts

Jennifer, a second grader, chose to write
about a rooster because she likes its colorful
feathers. She also likes to watch TV and make
jewelry. When Jennifer grows up, she wants
to be a doctor.

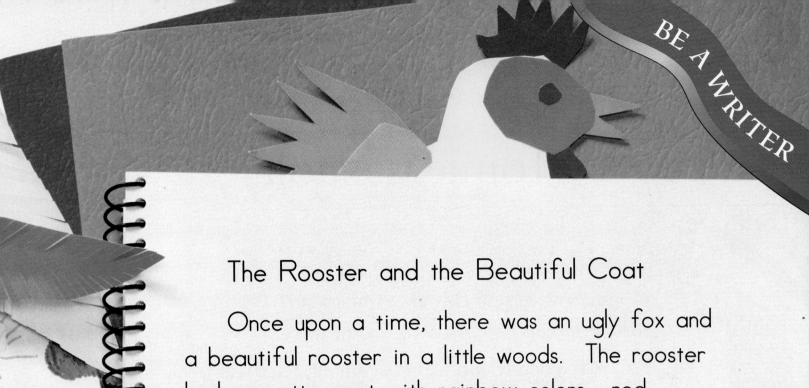

## The Rooster and the Beautiful Coat

Once upon a time, there was an ugly fox and a beautiful rooster in a little woods. The rooster had a pretty coat with rainbow colors: red, yellow, purple, orange, and green. It had round spots that shone in the sun and glittered like little stars at night. The coat was very warm and soft like the wool of the lamb. The rooster put some flowers on the coat every morning and made it smell like perfume in the breeze.

The fox borrowed the beautiful coat of the rooster because he had to go to a party. He said he would give it back in the morning. The next morning the rooster went to the river and had delicious worms as his breakfast.

He waited for the fox to give him back his coat. He waited one day, two days, but the fox never came. Every morning he shouted "cock-a-doodle-do" to ask the fox to bring back the coat.

233

# A Message from
# Tomie dePaola

Did you know that there are lots of stories about how certain flowers came to be? *The Legend of the Indian Paintbrush* is one of these.

My good friend from Wyoming, Pat Henry, wrote me a letter asking me to retell and illustrate one of the stories about the Indian Paintbrush, which is the state flower of Wyoming. She sent me three or four different stories. I liked one better than the others because it was about a Native American artist who tried to match the colors of the sunset.

Everyone has his or her own way of telling stories. When I find old stories that I like, I retell them, which means that I add some things and tell the story with what writers call their "voice." That means I tell the story the way *I* tell stories.

I especially like to retell old legends because I think the old legends have something interesting for people of all ages and all cultures.

# ❖ The Legend of ❖
# the Indian Paintbrush

retold and illustrated by
## Tomie dePaola

Many years ago when the People traveled the Plains and lived in a circle of teepees, there was a boy who was smaller than the rest of the children in the tribe. No matter how hard he tried, he couldn't keep up with the other boys who were always riding, running, shooting their bows, and wrestling to prove their strength. Sometimes his mother and father worried for him.

But the boy, who was called Little Gopher, was not without a gift of his own. From an early age, he made toy warriors from scraps of leather and pieces of wood and he loved to decorate smooth stones with the red juices from berries he found in the hills.

The wise shaman of the tribe understood that Little Gopher had a gift that was special. "Do not struggle, Little Gopher. Your path will not be the same as the others. They will grow up to be warriors. Your place among the People will be remembered for a different reason."

And in a few years when Little Gopher was older,
he went out to the hills alone to think about becoming
a man, for this was the custom of the tribe. And it was
there that a Dream-Vision came to him.

The sky filled with clouds and out of them came
a young Indian maiden and an old grandfather. She
carried a rolled-up animal skin and he carried a brush
made of fine animal hairs and pots of paints.

The grandfather spoke. "My son, these are the tools by which you shall become great among your People. You will paint pictures of the deeds of the warriors and the visions of the shaman, and the People shall see them and remember them forever."

The maiden unrolled a pure white buckskin and placed it on the ground. "Find a buckskin as white as this," she told him. "Keep it and one day you will paint a picture that is as pure as the colors in the evening sky."

And as she finished speaking, the clouds cleared
and a sunset of great beauty filled the sky. Little
Gopher looked at the white buckskin and on it he saw
colors as bright and beautiful as those made by the
setting sun.

Then the sun slowly sank behind the hills, the sky
grew dark, and the Dream-Vision was over. Little
Gopher returned to the circle of the People.

The next day he began to make soft brushes from the hairs of different animals and stiff brushes from the hair of the horses' tails.  He gathered berries and flowers and rocks of different colors and crushed them to make his paints.

He collected the skins of animals, which the warriors brought home from their hunts. He stretched the skins on wooden frames and pulled them until they were tight.

And he began to paint pictures of great hunts and great deeds . . .

and of great Dream-Visions so that the People would
always remember.

But even as he painted, Little Gopher sometimes longed to put aside his brushes and ride out with the warriors. But always he remembered his Dream-Vision and he did not go with them.

Many months ago, he had found his pure white buckskin, but it remained empty because he could not find the colors of the sunset. He used the brightest flowers, the reddest berries, and the deepest purples from the rocks, and still his paintings never satisfied him. They looked dull and dark.

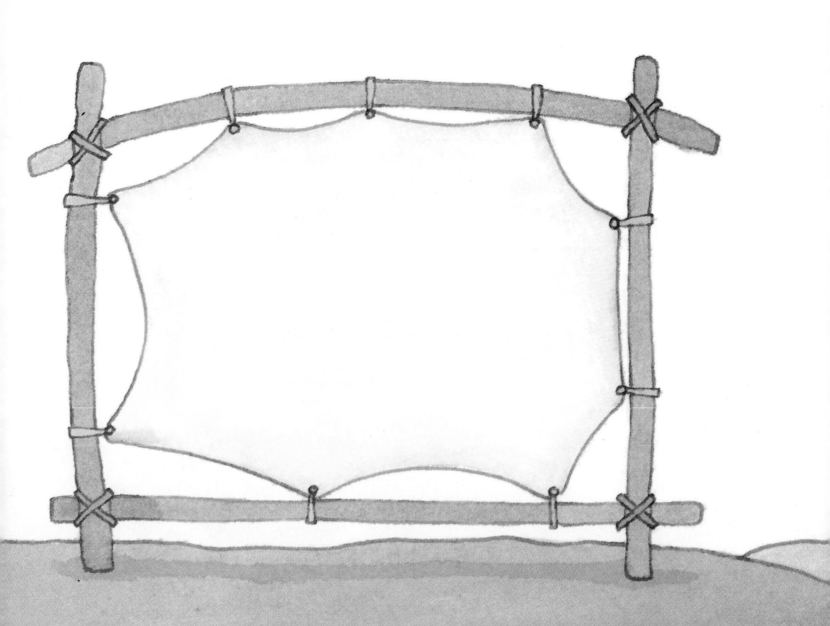

He began to go to the top of a hill each evening
and look at the colors that filled the sky to try and
understand how to make them. He longed to share the
beauty of his Dream-Vision with the People.

But he never gave up trying, and every morning when he awoke, he took out his brushes and his pots of paints and created the stories of the People with the tools he had.

One night as he lay awake, he heard a voice calling to
him. "Because you have been faithful to the People and
true to your gift, you shall find the colors you are seeking.
Tomorrow take the white buckskin and go to the
place where you watch the sun in the evening. There on
the ground you will find what you need."

The next evening as the sun began to go down,
Little Gopher put aside his brushes and went to the
top of the hill as the colors of the sunset spread across
the sky.

And there, on the ground all around him, were
brushes filled with paint, each one a color of the sunset.
Little Gopher began to paint quickly and surely, using
one brush, then another.

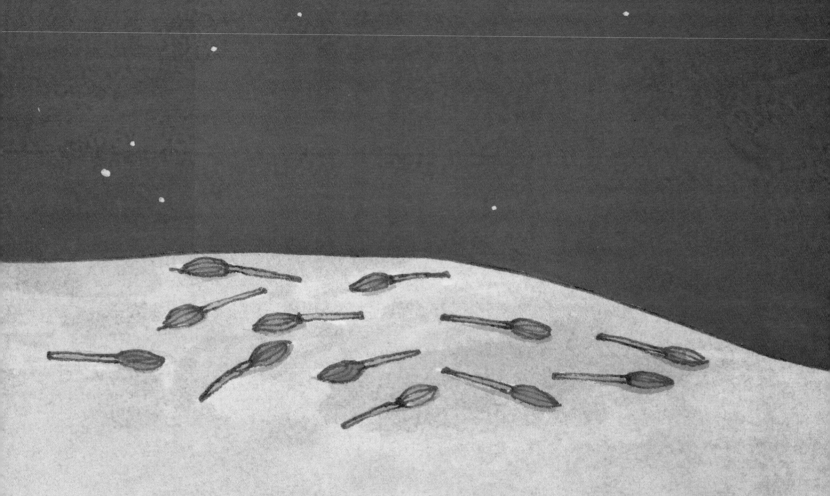

And as the colors in the sky began to fade, Little
Gopher gazed at the white buckskin and he was happy.
He had found the colors of the sunset. He carried his
painting down to the circle of the People, leaving the
brushes on the hillside.

And the next day, when the People awoke, the hill was ablaze with color, for the brushes had taken root in the earth and multiplied into plants of brilliant reds, oranges and yellows.

And every spring from that time, the hills and meadows burst into bloom. And every spring, the People danced and sang the praises of Little Gopher who had painted for the People. And the People no longer called him Little Gopher, but He-Who-Brought-the-Sunset-to-the-Earth.

# Retell the Tale

Little Gopher's story has been told over and over for many years. How would *you* tell the story? Work alone or with a partner. Choose a way to share your ideas.

- Draw pictures of some of the important scenes. Retell the story as you show your pictures.

- Collect props for the story and put them in the pockets of a story apron or in a cardboard box. Pull out the props as you retell the story.

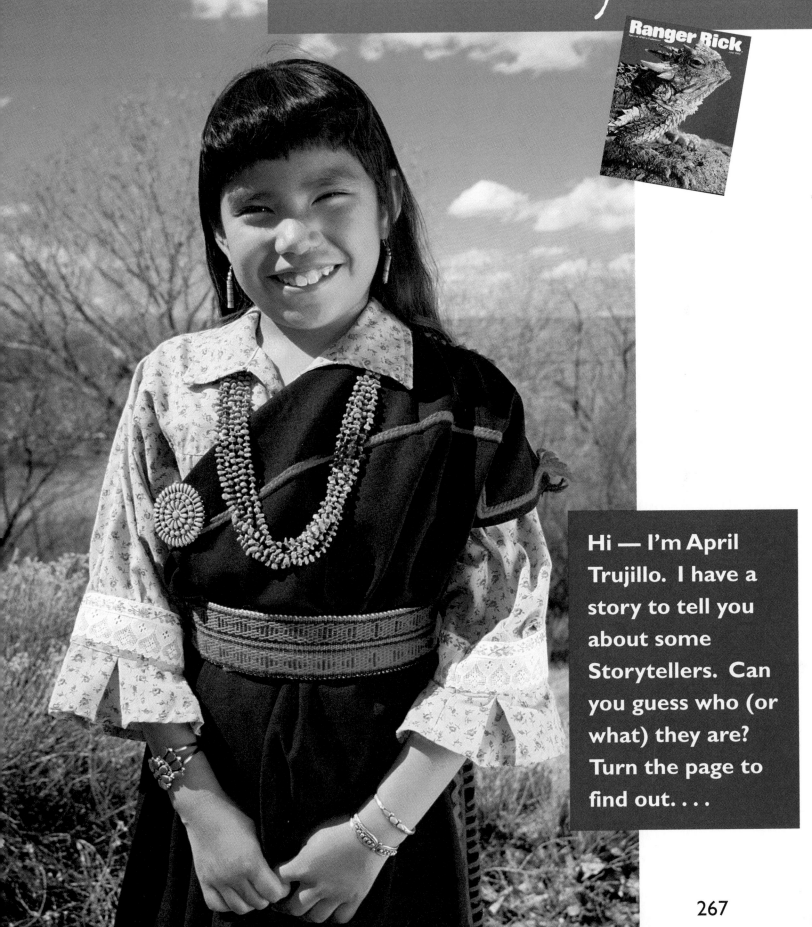

Ranger Rick

Hi — I'm April Trujillo. I have a story to tell you about some Storytellers. Can you guess who (or what) they are? Turn the page to find out. . . .

267

For me there is a special time at the end of every day. After I've finished my homework and chores, I get ready for bed. But I don't like to go to sleep without hearing a story about the past from one of my grandparents. It's amazing how many stories they know by heart!

They tell the legends of my Native American ancestors — fantastic stories of brave people and wise animals. I also like to hear stories of what life was like at their *pueblos* (PWEB-loze) when they were young. (Pueblo is a Spanish word for village, and we are called Pueblo Indians.) When they tell a story, I feel as if everything they say is happening around me.

Digging out the clay near our pueblo is hard work. We carry buckets of clay back to my grandfather's truck. I really like being outdoors with my grandfather. Along the way, he tells me all about the plants and animals we see. Once we found the tracks of a mountain lion!

268

**When clay comes from the ground, it's as hard as a rock and very dry (left).**

**My grandfather softens the clay with water. Then he adds white sand (below), which will make the clay stronger.**

Not only are my grandparents good at telling stories, but they also *make* Storytellers.

Make them? Yes, the Cochiti (KO-chit-ee) Pueblo where I live is famous for making clay figures called Storytellers. People come from all around the world to our pueblo near Santa Fe, New Mexico, to buy the Storytellers we make.

My grandmother learned to make Storytellers and other clay pottery from *her* mother. Then she taught my mother how. But my mother died when I was three. So now my grandmother teaches me.

269

My grandmother shows me how to make the body of her favorite clay figure: the Storyteller. She forms the shapes of little children.

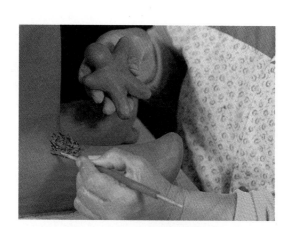

Then she scratches the wet clay on a part of the Storyteller's body.

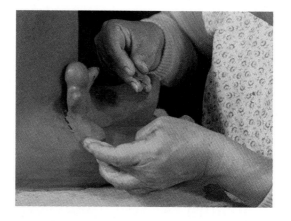

Finally, she attaches a child to the scratched part with bits of clay.

When the last child has been added, the Storyteller is left to dry. It sits in a warm corner of my grandmother's kitchen for many days.

My grandfather shows me how to sand our Storyteller figures. By sanding, he makes the surface of the clay smooth enough to paint.

We put our clay Storytellers on a grate, and my grandmother covers them with cow pies. Then we put some wood under the grate and lean more of it against the sides.

I'm glad that I'm learning all I can about making Storytellers. And someday I will tell my children and grandchildren the stories I've learned from my grandparents — my *real-life* storytellers!

The fire in this kiln will make the clay pottery much stronger.

This Storyteller is meant to look like my great-great-grandfather with a lap full of children. They are all listening as the Storyteller remembers a tale or sings a song about the old days.

# Be a Storyteller Like Judith Black

Judith Black loves to tell stories. Here she is telling the story "The Poor Unfortunate Man" to children at the Phoenix School in Salem, Massachusetts. You can tell stories too! Just read these tips from Judith Black.

**1.** Choose a story you like. It could be a folktale, a fairy tale, or a story that you made up. Some of the best stories you'll ever find are family stories. You might say to your mom, "Hey, Mom! Tell me a story about something that happened to you when you were little!" And she might tell you about a time she got in trouble or was embarrassed at school.

*"If you're telling a new story, and you're trying to learn it, make a movie of it in your imagination."*

*"The way you say something is as important as what you say. If it's a scary story, say it in a scary way."*

**2.** Think about how you will tell your story. If you're telling a new story, and you're trying to learn it, make a movie of it in your imagination. Try to see the story happening as you tell it. You can even draw a picture of each scene.

**3.** Have fun telling your story. Use your voice, your face, and your body to help you tell the story. The way you say something is as important as what you say. If it's a scary story, say it in a scary way. Let your body feel scared, and let your face look scared.

**4.** Tell your story to some friends or relatives. When you share your story, people will want to tell you their stories. It's like a circle. The stories will go round and round.

# GLOSSARY

This glossary can help you find out the meanings of some of the words in this book. The meanings given are the meanings of the words as they are used in the book. Sometimes a second meaning is also given.

## A

**ablaze**  Glowing or shining very brightly: *At the end of the evening, the sky was **ablaze** with fireworks.*

**admire**  To enjoy looking at something: *Matt **admired** my brand-new bike.*

**amusement park**  A place where there are rides to go on and other fun things to do: *We rode on the merry-go-round at the **amusement park.***

**ancient**  Very old: *We saw the **ancient** bones of a dinosaur.*

**aquarium**  A glass tank filled with water in which fish and other water animals are kept: *Amanda has many brightly colored fish swimming in her **aquariums.***

**aquarium**

**asteroid**  A tiny planet that circles around the sun.  There are thousands of asteroids in space, but most are in the area between Mars and Jupiter.

**B**

**bamboo**   A very tall grass that looks like a tree.  Bamboo stems can be used to make furniture and fishing poles.

**bargain**   Something bought at a low price: *At five dollars, this shirt is a **bargain.***

**batch**   An amount made at one time: *Aunt Nancy baked a **batch** of cookies.*

**batch**

**beak**   **1.** The part of a bird's mouth that is hard and ends in a point.  **2.** A hard, curved part that is like a beak in the mouth of other animals: *The octopus cracked the crab's shell with its **beak.***

**bored**   Not interested: *The movie **bored** me because nothing happened in it.*

**C**

**change**   **1.** Coins: *Do you need **change** for the bus?*  **2.** To become different: *Many leaves **change** color in the fall.*

**clever**   Smart: *Max thought of a **clever** way to solve the problem.*

**coin**   A kind of money.  Coins are usually round and made of metal.  Pennies, nickels, dimes, and quarters are all coins.

**coin**

**confess**   To admit to having done something: *I **confess** that I lost your book.*

**count**   To add up: *I will **count** the money in my piggy bank today.*

**custom**   Something that the members of a group usually do: *It is a **custom** in our town to have a parade on the Fourth of July.*

**decorate**   To make something look pretty: *The baker will **decorate** the birthday cake with yellow roses.*

**deed**   An act: *Julia did a good **deed** by returning the lost wallet.*

**den**   An animal's home: *The bear was hiding in its **den.***

den

**diner**   A restaurant that usually has the shape of a railroad car: *David and his mother ate lunch at a **diner.***

diner

**double**   Two times the amount: *I will have twelve muffins instead of six if I **double** this recipe.*

**dough** A soft, thick mixture of water, flour, or other ingredients. Dough is used to make bread and other baked goods.

**dough**

**dusk** Early in the evening, just before it gets dark: *The streetlights in the city come on at **dusk.***

**embrace** To hug: *The kitten purred when Samantha **embraced** it.*

**embroidery** A piece of cloth with designs sewed onto it: *The **embroideries** hanging on the walls are beautiful.*

**embroidery**

**exactly** In every way: *I took Sasha's book by mistake because it looks **exactly** like mine.*

**exchange** To give one thing for another: *Lori **exchanged** her apple for Kim's orange.*

279

**gift**   A special talent: *My friend has a **gift** for music.*

**grateful**   Thankful for a gift or a favor: *Mr. Ling was **grateful** when Beth walked his dog.*

**humble**   Simple, not fancy: *The **humble** cabin has only two rooms.*

**identical**   Looking just the same: *Gloria and I are **identical** twins.*

**identical twins**

**intelligence**   The power to learn and think: *The dog showed his **intelligence** by doing every trick I asked him to do.*

**interrupt**   To start to talk while someone else is speaking: *Please don't **interrupt** me while I'm telling my story.*

**invent**   To make something that has never been made before: *Who **invented** the telephone?*

**keen**   Very sharp, especially in seeing, hearing, tasting, or smelling: *Tigers have a **keen** sense of smell.*

**knead**   To mix something by folding, stretching, or pressing it: *Gary **kneaded** the pizza dough with his hands.*

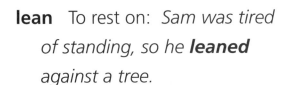

**lean**  To rest on: *Sam was tired of standing, so he leaned against a tree.*

**pale**  Light in color: *Ron's cat is black, but mine is pale gray.*

**paralyze**  To cause a living thing to be unable to move: *The octopus paralyzed the clam with poison from its mouth.*

**platter**  A large dish or plate for serving food: *Dad cut the meat and put the slices on a platter.*

**platter**

**plentiful**  More than enough: *Our market has a plentiful supply of dog food.*

**prey**  An animal hunted by another animal for food: *Chickens are the prey of wolves.*

**pumps**  Shoes for a girl or woman: *Mom took off her pumps and put on slippers.*

**pumps**

**recess**  Time out from something: *I played on the swings during recess at school.*

**recognize**  To know from having seen before: *When Chen wore a mask, I didn't recognize him.*

281

**record** A disk with grooves. When a record is played on a special machine called a phonograph, you can hear music.

**record**

**roller coaster** A ride in an amusement park in which cars go up and down tracks with sharp turns: *Yolanda thought the* **roller coaster** *went too fast, but I enjoyed the ride.*

**roller coaster**

**S**

**satisfy** To please: *José was* **satisfied** *with his report.*

**savings** Money saved up: *Olga spent most of her* **savings** *on a new bike.*

**scared** Frightened: *The cat was* **scared** *when it saw the dog.*

**scent** A smell: *A skunk gives off a terrible* **scent** *when it sprays.*

**scientist** A person whose job it is to learn more about the world and the things in it: *Some* **scientists** *study animals.*

**shock** A very sudden upset: *It was a* **shock** *to hear that Melissa moved away.*

**shoulder** The part of the body between the neck and the arm: *The straps of a backpack go over your* **shoulders**.

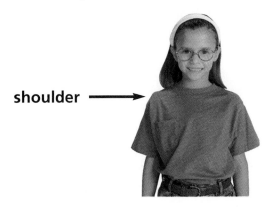

shoulder

**shower** To sprinkle or spray: *My brother* **showered** *me with water from the hose.*

**sofa** A long seat with a back and arms: *My little sister sits next to me on the* **sofa** *when I read to her.*

sofa

**sparkle** To shine brightly: *Millions of stars* **sparkled** *in the sky.*

**spoiled** Ruined: *Kevin* **spoiled** *my painting when he spilled milk on it.*

**suction cup** A soft plastic cup that sticks to something else. Some people put suction cups on windows and hang pictures and other objects from them.

**suction cups**

**swallow** To make food pass from one's mouth into the stomach: *Molly chewed the meat before she* **swallowed** *it.*

283

# T

**tip** An extra amount of money given to someone for doing a good job. When people eat out, they often leave a tip for the person who serves them.

**tool** Something people use to help them do work: *Brushes and paints are an artist's* **tools.**

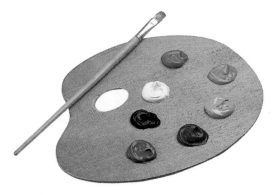

**tools**

**twice as much** Two times more: *I get* **twice as much** *for my allowance as my younger brother does.*

# V

**velvet** A soft, thick material: *Carol tied her hair back with a* **velvet** *bow.*

# W

**warrior** Someone who fights in a war: *Long ago, some* **warriors** *used bows and arrows for fighting.*

**webbed** Having a fold of skin that connects the toes or arms. Frogs, otters, and ducks have webbed feet. Octopuses have webbed arms.

**webbed**

# ACKNOWLEDGMENTS

"3-D Picture Pop-Outs," from December 1994 *Ranger Rick* magazine. Copyright © 1994 by the National Wildlife Federation. Reprinted by permission.

*A Chair for My Mother*, written and illustrated by Vera B. Williams. Copyright © 1982 by Vera B. Williams. Reprinted by permission of Greenwillow Books, an imprint of William Morrow & Company.

*An Octopus Is Amazing*, by Patricia Lauber, illustrated by Holly Keller. Text copyright © 1990 by Patricia Lauber. Illustrations copyright © 1990 by Holly Keller. Reprinted by permission of HarperCollins Publishers.

"Apple Volcanoes" and "Pretzels," from *Kids in the Kitchen*, by Micah Pulleyn and Sara Bracken. Copyright © 1994 by Altamont Press. Reprinted by permission of Sterling Publishing Company.

Selection from "Can You Beat These Guinness Records?" by Karen Romano Young, from September 1993 *3-2-1 Contact* magazine. Copyright © 1993 by the Children's Television Workshop. Reprinted by permission.

Selection from *I Wonder Why Triceratops Had Horns and Other Questions About Dinosaurs,* by Rod Theodorou. Copyright © 1994 by Grisewood & Dempsey Ltd. Reprinted by permission of Kingfisher Books.

"Incredible Recycling Facts," from *50 Simple Things Kids Can Do to Save the Earth,* by John Javna. Copyright © 1990 by John Javna. Reprinted by permission of Universal Press Syndicate.

"Invitation," from *There Was a Place and Other Poems,* by Myra Cohn Livingston. Copyright © 1988 by Myra Cohn Livingston. Reprinted by permission of Margaret K. McElderry Books, an imprint of Simon & Schuster Children's Publishing Division.

Selections from "Incredible Kids!" from *National Geographic World* magazine. "Amazing Grace," from December 1994 issue. "Play Ball," from November 1990 issue. "Uplifting Story," from August 1993 issue. "Safety First," from October 1993 issue. Copyright © 1990, 1993, 1994 by *National Geographic World*. *World* is the official magazine for Junior Members of the National Geographic Society. Reprinted by permission.

*The Legend of the Indian Paintbrush*, written and illustrated by Tomie dePaola. Copyright © 1988 by Tomie dePaola. Reprinted by permission of G.P. Putnam's Sons.

"My Family," by Delia Spotted Bear, from *Rising Voices: Writings of Young Native Americans,* selected by Arlene B. Hirschfelder and Beverly R. Singer. Copyright © 1992 by Arlene B. Hirschfelder and Beverly R. Singer. Reprinted by permission of Delia Spotted Bear.

*Now One Foot, Now the Other*, written and illustrated by Tomie dePaola. Copyright © 1981 by Tomie dePaola. Reprinted by permission of G.P. Putnam's Sons.

"Seeing Double," from July 1990 *National Geographic World.* Copyright © 1990 by *National Geographic World. World* is the official magazine for Junior Members of the National Geographic Society. Reprinted by permission.

"The Storyteller," from *Pueblo Storyteller,* by Diane Hoyt-Goldsmith. Copyright © 1991 by Diane Hoyt-Goldsmith. Reprinted by permission of Holiday House, Inc. Cover from June 1993 *Ranger Rick* magazine. Copyright © 1993 by the National Wildlife Federation. Reprinted by permission.

*To Friendship,* painting by Mr. Amos Ferguson accompanying the poem "To Friendship" from *Under the Sunday Tree* by Eloise Greenfield. Text copyright © 1988 by Eloise Greenfield. Paintings copyright © 1988 by Amos Ferguson. Reprinted by permission of HarperCollins Publishers.

*Too Many Tamales*, by Gary Soto, illustrated by Ed Martinez. Text copyright © 1993 by Gary Soto. Illustrations © 1993 by Ed Martinez. Reprinted by permission of G.P. Putnam's Sons.

*Two of Everything*, retold and illustrated by Lily Toy Hong. Copyright © 1993 by Lily Toy Hong. Reprinted by permission of Albert Whitman & Company.

*What Happened to Patrick's Dinosaurs?* by Carol Carrick, illustrated by Donald Carrick. Text copyright © 1986 by Carol Carrick. Illustrations copyright © 1986 by Donald Carrick. Reprinted by permission of Houghton Mifflin Company. All rights reserved.

"What's It Like to Be in the Circus?" from April 1994 *Sesame Street Magazine.* Copyright © 1994 by the Children's Television Workshop. Reprinted by permission.

Special thanks to the following teachers whose students' compositions appear in the Be a Writer features in this level: Kimberly English, Mae C. Jemison Academy, Detroit, Michigan; Jane En-Mi Kim, Creek Valley Elementary School, Edina, Minnesota; Marie Wong, Harvard Kent School, Charlestown, Massachusetts.

# CREDITS

**Illustration** **17–34** Vera B. Williams; **41–63** Tomie dePaola; **68** Julie Downing; **72–102** Ed Martinez; **111** Fred Schrier; **116** title by Artillery Studios; **118–146** Donald Carrick; **148–149** Karen Barnes/Wood Ronsaville Harlin Inc.; **157–180** Holly Keller; **195–223** Lily Toy Hong; **225–231** Francisco X. Mora; **236–265** Tomie dePaola

**Assignment Photography** **118, 147, 182–183, 184–185** (background), **186** (background), **194, 195, 224, 232–233, 234–235** (background); **266** Banta Digital Group; **112–113, 114–115, 273, 274–275,** Kindra Clineff; **235** Suki Coughlin; **14–15, 35** (background), **36–37, 40–41** (background), **42, 64, 69, 70–71** (background), **104** (background), **106–107** (background), **116–117** (background), **154–155** Tony Scarpetta; **12–13, 35** (inset), **103, 105** (insets), **106** (inset), **107** (insets), **181, 185** (inset), **186** (insets), **190–191, 192–193** Tracey Wheeler; **17, 72** Glenn Kremer; **156–157** (background) Dave Desroches